SILENT SPRINGS
THE PANTHER

SILENT SPRINGS THE PANTHER

HISTORIC ACCOUNTS OF MICHIGAN BIG CAT ATTACKS

AARON J. VESELENAK

MISSION POINT PRESS

Readers are encouraged to go to MissionPointPress.com to contact the author or to find information on how to buy this book in bulk at a discounted rate.

Published by Mission Point Press

MISSION POINT PRESS

2554 Chandler Rd.
Traverse City, MI 49696
(231) 421-9513
MissionPointPress.com

ISBN: 978-1-961302-47-1

Library of Congress Control Number: 2024907036

Printed in the United States of America

Dedicated to my own calico panther Matilda, a.k.a. "Tilly," who recently passed on (as of this publishing). At just shy of 7, you left Dad and the rest of your kitty siblings and nephews way too soon, girl. We miss your pure love and playfulness terribly. Until we meet again…

Contents

Part V A Doubtful Disappearance

Part VI Modern-Day Proof the Panther Still Prowls Michigan

Prologue

This prologue is written to address some very important concerns of mine over the subject matter of this book. First, and most importantly, I very much wish to avoid creating or solidifying an unfavorable impression of *Felis concolor*, i.e., panther, puma, mountain lion, cougar, etc. among the readership. I love the big cat (all felines in fact, big or small, wild or tame) and the last thing I'd ever want to do is cause persons to become loathsome and/or fearful of this beautiful animal due to the fact it is an extremely powerful creature that can do great harm, and on occasion has actually attacked humans—resulting in serious injury or death.

Then why produce a work bringing to light accounts of panther aggression against people? The answer, simply, is because their fierce actions against man, though rare, are a part of the animal's overall existence. To deny the potential danger or harm from this particular member of our native fauna would be dishonest and disingenuous. All truths, in my opinion, need to come out, ugly or beautiful, or anywhere in between.

So it is with this cat. However, I cannot stress enough that the panther's depredations on humans are, and have been, rare— exceedingly rare. If this is true, how can there be so many accounts of serious or even deadly attacks on people? The apparent inconsistency is answered via the inherent contradiction within the field of statistics. There exists the phenomenon whereby something measured can be numerically sufficient or even high, but percentage-wise low, or in fact, tiny. To truly gauge the amount of something—anything—one must put it into perspective or its proper proportion.

This is needed with panther attacks on humans. Proportionality or perspective is needed to be fair to the animal. One must balance the number of known cougar attacks over the years with the many times the big puss was spotted just casually observing people, within assault range, but remained passive the whole while. Or of the numerous instances the cat had a surprise encounter with humans only to traipse away. And on how many occasions did it occur historically whereby people were in the large cat's close physical presence but were completely oblivious, precisely because the given panther made no move against them? Over the long breadth of time these unknown but very real incidents have to number in the tens of thousands, if not millions! Perspective, proportionality, percentages—whatever one wants to call it—must be considered to truly be objective, and therefore just, to the puma.

Another issue I feel necessary to address is my reason for noting historic panther attacks on humans in other states of the United States. If the book is about Michigan's dangerous or deadly mountain lion encounters, why is there so much mention of and attention paid to cougar assaults that happened far distant from the Great Lakes State? The reason lies in the fact that there have been similar or near-identical experiences of Michigan big cat incidents with those that have taken place in other regions of the country. The animal's behavior, aggressive or benign, is better understood if near-matching occurrences are recognized and brought to light.

Finally, I'd like to confront the question of veracity or truthfulness. It is known that news reporting has been, and historical records often are, proven erroneous, regardless of the subject matter. The false information is usually the result of honest mistakes. Often enough, however, untrue stories or accounts are produced deliberately, i.e., what we refer to today as "fake news." Whatever the cause of false stories—accidental error or purposeful misrepresentation—reporting on the Western Hemisphere's panther has never been any different from other issues or topics, and therefore is not immune from the plague of serious mistruths.

With that being said, to be an honest researcher and author, it behooves me to admit that some of the panther/human encounters covered in this work may be fictitious, or if not outright false, may be to a certain degree embellished. A seeker and presenter of truth therefore must do his or her best to dig deep in order to maximize the accuracy of one's reporting. And I can assure the reader that I have done just that—shoveled deep—to the point of exhaustion. Being fallible though, this author may have missed certain articles, reports, news stories, etc. which retracted or debunked what was or has been presented as truth.

Because of the possibility of either slight or profound error, I sincerely invite any reader to spend some time delving deeper to further investigate any particular panther incident from Michigan or other states brought forth within these pages. In all honesty, if anything I've written is later shown to be inaccurate or false, a service has been rendered no matter the initial disappointment to me. In the end, I won't be offended, but rather grateful, for having had the truth come out.

Due to my concern over potential falsehoods, this author makes mention of a couple of real cases as examples of the press reporting incidents of either wrongful speculation or outright false claims regarding panther violence against people. Please see the epilogue of this publication.

Having now addressed these concerns, my hope is that you will have an interesting and entertaining read.

Cordially,
Aaron J. Veselenak March 2022

Prelude

The First Americans and the Panther

Unfortunately, there is very little to bring forth regarding historical accounts of the Native Peoples of Michigan and the big cat we
know as the "panther." So many oral histories have been lost with the
passage of time, and there is little mention of experiences between the
feline and first Michiganders in the written record. However, one
can surmise, minus such records, that over the passing centuries and
millennia, the earliest inhabitants of the Great Lakes State had thousands upon thousands of encounters with the cougar.

Most, by far, we can assume were uneventful, if not outright
benign. Others, for sure, were violent—whether it was the humans
initiating the conflict, or the big cat through natural predation.
Either way, there is little out there to go by.

What do we have? Well, we know what the panther, i.e., cougar, mountain lion, puma, etc. was called by the Ojibwa Tribe of
Michigan and surrounding states. In his *A Dictionary of the Otchipwe*

Silent Springs the Panther

Language, Frederic Baraga records the general name of "cat" as "gaja-gens," and "minons." Baraga became the first Catholic bishop in the Upper Peninsula of Michigan and preached among the Natives.

This Native group (more commonly called "Chippewa" but more accurately pronounced "Ojibwa") knew enough about cats to differentiate between the three separate species dwelling in Michigan and surrounding regions. The "lion" (via translation almost certainly meant what we today know as "panther") was named "mishibiji" by the Ojibwa. The bobcat, in the early years of European settlement, was referred to as "wildcat" by the whites. However, to the Ojibwa, the "bobcat" or "wildcat" was called "essiban." The lynx, which can easily be mistaken for the bobcat, and vice versa, was named "bisew" in the Ojibwa tongue.

Sadly, whatever the encounters were between the cat (of whatever species) and the Ojibwa have largely, if not completely, been lost in time. What other Native tribes had to say is scant too, if not lost. Two translations of the name of the famous Shawnee leader Tecumseh are that of "crouching panther" or "leaping panther." Another says, "shooting star." Tecumseh was from the region that would eventually become the state of Ohio. However, the heroic leader of Indian forces prior to and during the War of 1812 spent much time in southeastern Michigan engaged in efforts to drive American settlers out.

Lake Erie, one of the world's largest inland lakes and one of the five Great Lakes of North America, touches southeastern Michigan. This immense body of water was named after the Erie Tribe. These Native people lived along the southern shore of the big lake that bears their name—in what became regions of the U.S. states of Ohio, Pennsylvania, and New York. The Erie were decimated and nearly completely wiped out by the much more powerful Iroquois Nation. Erie meant "panther" in the Iroquois language. This ill-fated Native group was also known as "Cat Nation." Presumably the Iroquois had named this tribe "Erie" prior to vanquishing them, due to the large number of big cats inhabiting the same part of North America.

Getting back to Michigan proper, an actual panther specimen was discovered among the Natives of the state, albeit posthumously for both. During late October of 1966, an Indian burial was found in a plowed wheat field in Taymouth Township in southern Saginaw County. The interment site was within a few hundred feet of the Flint River. Subsequent excavation in November of 1966 revealed the skeletal remains of four Native children. The burial was considered rare due to the fact that it was determined to be a secondary grave, with nearly all postcranial bones (femurs, tibias, fibulas, humeri, radiuses, and ulnas) having been methodically broken into two or three pieces prior to placement.

Among the human bones was the skull of a cougar. The scientists associated with this specific excavation and overall study speculated that the skull may have had its pelt attached to it at the moment of burial, serving as a "skin robe" wrapped around the remains of the Native children. Skin robes had been found within other secondary burials in the Upper Great Lakes region. Additional speculation surmised the panther head may have had a ceremonial purpose.

Questions arise that can never be answered but still need to be asked. Was the cougar skull placed among the deceased Native children meant to honor them or, more importantly, protect their innocent souls in the afterlife? Or was the specimen simply placed as a matter of convenience (meaning if a hide was originally attached to the panther skull, it was merely used to wrap the children's remains for a tidier burial)?

Maybe there was a quite sinister reason for the panther skull (with or without skin) being placed in the children's grave. Perhaps the children were all slain by the puma. It seems highly unlikely that even an adult panther would be able to kill so many children in the same time frame. Wouldn't one or two of the youngsters have been able to take to their heels and escape during an attack?

That all the Native kids were fatally preyed upon in the same moment by this particular big cat is unlikely. Impossible though? No. So, it is plausible that the panther in question did kill the four young and possibly unattended Native children, and was therefore subsequently pursued and done away with by tribal adults. This side of Heaven, those interested in knowing why the children and panther were put together for eternity will never learn the real reason.

Perhaps over time more information will be brought to light, illuminating some of the currently unknown but quite obvious incredibly high number of meetings between the Native Peoples of Michigan and the American panther.

This cougar skull was discovered among the remains of four Native children at a pre-Columbian burial site unearthed in the fall of 1966 in Taymouth Township, Saginaw County, Michigan. The panther cranium and children's bones have since been repatriated with the Indigenous People of the Saginaw Valley. *Photocopy courtesy of Michael J. Hambacher, Staff Archaeologist, State (of Michigan) Historic Preservation Office.*

SILENT SPRINGS
THE PANTHER

PART I
PIONEER ENCOUNTERS

Millicent Dexter's Wild Ride

Chapter 1

The Chase Is On

In June of 1895, Julia Dexter Stannard, while addressing the Washtenaw County, Michigan, Pioneer Society, gave a dramatic account of a very close encounter her mother had with a panther many years earlier, circa 1828. Stannard's parents, Samuel W. and Millicent Dexter, were early pioneers of Washtenaw County and leading citizens of the town of Dexter, Michigan. Julia's father, who came from wealth and prominence, was the founder of the town which bears his name (see sidebar 1). Together, Samuel and Millicent had eight children, all of whom lived to adulthood. Julia, born in 1837, was their fifth child. Granddaughter Katharine, daughter of son Wirt, became nationally renowned through her support for women's issues (see sidebar 2).

Samuel W. Dexter was a county judge and held many other important positions in the infant community—one of which was

Dexter postmaster. Young wife Millicent, only 16 years old when the two wed, was made to be deputy postmaster in 1828.

Occasionally it was necessary for Judge Dexter to stay in the town of Ann Arbor overnight to work on business of the court. When this was expected, Millicent would accompany her husband in the morning and return alone in the late afternoon, hauling mail back to the Dexter post office while riding on horseback.

Once, while the court was in session, Mrs. Dexter was about to return to Dexter from Ann Arbor but was delayed by a sudden and powerful storm. When finally able to make the familiar but not-so-easy journey back from whence she came, Julia's father saw his wife off, saying reassuringly to her, "You will soon be home." With that, Mrs. Dexter shot off like an arrow on her pony. Woman and beast, with their cargo of mail, followed an old, well-worn Native trail across the hills and through "dark woods."

"In a deep ravine," related Julia Dexter Stannard to her fellow pioneer club members, "the horse sprang aside, snorting with fear, as the fiery eyes and hot breath of a hungry panther were upon the rider's face. It was a wild race between the trembling, terror-stricken horse and the fiery-eyed, panting panther. With the sight of the lights in the windows at home the panther gave up the chase, and the horse, foam-covered and tired, was led away to the stable."

Cats of every kind engage in the chase. It is within their nature. Whether to secure a kill in order to feast or for sport, the chase is part of what makes a cat a cat.

Enoch Lawrence (or "E. L.") Barrett traveled with his wife and several small children to homestead on 160 acres near Paw Paw Village, Van Buren County, Michigan, in 1833. There was not yet a single framed house in Van Buren County, but the hardy man soon went to work and is credited with having erected the very first one on a village lot in the little town.

Michigan historian Franklin Ellis wrote of Barrett: "He drove the first team from Paw Paw to Little Prairie Ronde (a large expanse of prairie near what became Kalamazoo, Michigan), and upon his return experienced the exciting sensation of being chased by a panther and a pack of wolves." Details of this particular large feline and canine encounter forever evade us, but for lovers of history, we are grateful to have at least this much.

A newspaper article from October 1929 covered the local citizens of Van Buren County celebrating their county's centennial anniversary by organizing and launching a mammoth parade. The unknown author of the piece made mention of an Indian named Jim as having been killed and partially eaten by a panther many years earlier in a thickly wooded area known as the "North Woods" (north of the town of Paw Paw). Neither the exact nor approximate year of the man's attack and demise were provided.

Another newspaper article from January 1913 cited a Mr. O'Dell, who spoke of Paw Paw's early years. The fellow recounted that as a

Millicent Bond Dexter in her middle-aged and elderly years.
Photos courtesy of the Dexter Area Historical Society, Dexter, Michigan.

kid he used to travel on occasion with his father, a physician, to administer to the health needs of local citizens. One evening the pair rode in a horse-drawn buggy to visit a sick client. En route the two were startled by a rustling among the leaves and branches of a tree, but the source of the noise could not be ascertained as darkness hindered their vision. Soon, however, both father and son spotted a pair of eyes resembling "balls of fire." An animal, described by O'Dell as either a panther or wildcat, leaped over the buggy's rear wheels. The boy was so frightened he could barely move. The harrowing event also took place within the "North Woods"—a two-and-a-half-mile tract of land north of the village of Paw Paw.

James B. Voddin was a "sturdy pioneer" of Burton Township in Genesee County, Michigan. Similar to most Michiganders of that time, the fellow was born elsewhere—in Stafford, Ontario County, New York. He entered the world on February 17, 1840. His father, Henry Voddin, emigrated from England to the United States at the age of 19, and eventually brought his wife and young children to Burton Township, Genesee County, Michigan, in 1845. The young family settled on section 14, approximately four miles south of Flint.

Young James Voddin, like virtually all pioneer children, worked strenuously to keep the family not just meagerly subsisting, but literally alive. While the boy's father was away from home on business, which was frequently the circumstance, James labored with his mother, Mary Delbridge Voddin. The two produced maple sugar, walking from tree to tree to drain sap. The work was tough, but not dangerous per se. However, on more than one occasion it actually became life-threatening, as the two were chased to their home a few times by wolves and once by a panther (early-to-mid 1850s).

The wolves were undoubtedly hungry and therefore out to kill. However, one can't necessarily say that about the cougar. Big cats will chase people or any other creature out of instinct, due to curiosity, independent of whatever their appetite is or amount of hunger they feel. Much more often than not, if something runs from a cat, the feline will quickly follow. So we don't actually know if pioneer mother and son were truly in danger when chased by the panther—though for the two family members, the reason for the massive cat's pursuit did not matter. They weren't going to stick around to experience the beast's intentions.

Husband and wife John C. and Parthena (Lawson) Rinehart were among the early settlers of Cass County, Michigan. They had six children, one of whom died in infancy—Thomas—in 1846. Exactly when the two arrived in the county is unclear, but John Rinehart's younger brother, Abraham Rinehart (1817–1895), had been a farmer in Cass County since 1840. John (June 15, 1814–February 20, 1881) and Parthena (March 15, 1821–July 27, 1910) were also farmers, with John additionally working for brother Abe as head sawyer at the latter's sawmill. The sturdy couple, like all homesteaders, toiled extremely hard while facing abundant difficulties. One particular dangerous encounter stands out.

While returning home from religious services in Newberg one Sunday afternoon, Mr. and Mrs. Rinehart caught the eye of a prowling panther. The two rode either in a horse-drawn wagon or buggy—likely a buggy because only a single horse is mentioned in the account's narration. The big cat began to stalk the couple, who soon became aware of its presence. For several miles the panther continued behind them, even encircling the unnerved sojourners. Their horse was terrified and became nearly uncontrollable every time the cougar let out a "blood-curdling" cry.

The Rineharts felt an attack by the trailing and (at times) flanking cat was imminent. Luckily though, or perhaps by the grace of God, their fears went unrealized. The panther strolled off as the nerve-wracked churchgoers and panicky horse neared the waters known as Birch Lake.

One can only speculate why the panther followed man, woman,

JOHN RINEHART.

Cass County, Michigan, pioneer residents John C. Rinehart (1814–1881), and wife Parthena (Lawson) Rinehart (1821–1910) were trailed for several miles—even encircled—by a wild panther one Sunday afternoon as they rode home in their horse-drawn buggy after attending church service. The puma eventually ran off, much to the relief of the fear-stricken, unarmed couple. Was the big cat sizing up the two humans and their beast of burden for an attack, or was it merely just being curious as cats of all types are wont to be? *Sketch from www.findagrave.com*

and beast of burden for as long as it did—several miles in fact—on this particular occasion. Was the big cat famished and therefore contemplating attack? Or was the feline merely curious, as such critters are famously known to be?

As the Rineharts were spared attack, a person might think these questions moot. But are they really? After all, a wild, hungry beast is assuredly more dangerous than a curious one.

Reuben F. Gard was a pioneer child of Volinia Township, Cass County, Michigan. Though the historical record is vague, Reuben appears to be the son of Jonathon Gard and grandson of Joseph Gard (1774–1840). Grandfather Joseph came to Volinia Township in 1831 from Union City, Indiana, and previously from Ohio. However, the eldest Gard originally hailed from New Jersey, where he was born.

From Volinia Township, Joseph Gard moved to nearby Berrien County, Michigan, and dwelled there until his death in 1840. But some of the man's offspring stayed in Volinia, Cass County.

In that era of so long ago, friction matches were difficult to come by, so pioneer children were oftentimes sent to the closest neighboring homestead to obtain some if fires had died out in their home's fireplace. Young Reuben was sent afoot on just such a mission one "frosty morning" (year unknown). The dutiful son went to the house of a man, George Newton. On his way, the youth spotted a giant cat, hunkered down within the fork of a tree that leaned over the trail he walked upon. The boy excitedly reported his sighting to Mr. Newton.

An organized search for the panther quickly took place, and it was soon revealed that the "monster" had killed a colt owned by a Mr. D. C. Squires. Young Reuben Gard was said to have had a "narrow escape."

Though a narrow escape could very likely have been the situation for the youngster, the boy may never have been in any real danger at all. Maybe the cougar's appetite was satiated at the moment and it posed no threat. Or perhaps the cat was indeed hungry, but a natural instinct to avoid humans kept it at bay. As has been stated, almost certainly there have been thousands upon thousands of instances over the years when big cats eyed people of all ages and sizes, only to permanently retreat or just watch them from a distance in a curious, nonthreatening, innocuous manner. Thankfully this was the case with Reuben Gard.

Samuel W. Dexter. *Photo courtesy of the Dexter Area Historical Society, Dexter, Michigan.*

Samuel W. Dexter was born in Boston, Massachusetts, in 1792, the eldest son of Samuel and Catherine Gordon Dexter. Samuel the elder served as U.S. Secretary of War and U.S. Secretary of the Treasury under U.S. President John Adams.

As a young man, the younger Samuel attended Harvard University, graduating in 1812. He obtained a law degree three years later. After moving to Athens, New York, in 1816, Samuel married Amelia Augusta Prevost. The couple had two children— Samuel P. (1817–1849), and Augustine, born in 1820. Tragically, mother and daughter succumbed to severe illness. Both died in 1822.

In August of 1824, Mr. Dexter moved to Detroit. With a handsome sum of money, the adventurous man bought large tracts of land at several locations in the Territory of Michigan. Through his property purchases, Dexter helped establish several communities—Byron, in Shiawassee County; Dexter, the town which bears his name, in Washtenaw County; and Saginaw, in Saginaw County.

Returning to Massachusetts in 1825, Dexter married his second wife, Susan Dunham. Samuel brought his new bride to Michigan soon thereafter in 1826. The two lived in a log cabin while a frame house was being built in what would, in a matter of a few years, become the town of Dexter. The wealthy man also had a sawmill, gristmill, and a boarding house built to assist all of the locale's newcomers. When his frame house was completed, Samuel established a post office within it and also allowed members of several religious denominations to worship there.

Samuel W. Dexter was appointed chief justice of Washtenaw County in 1826 by Michigan territorial governor Lewis Cass, a Michigander of tremendous renown. Mr. Dexter served as judge until 1833. In 1827 he and Susan had a son, but not long after both the baby boy and mother died. So, in 1828 Dexter married his third wife, 16-year-old Millicent Bond. At the time Samuel was 36. Millicent had recently come to the Michigan Territory from Massachusetts with her widowed mother. Sam and Millicent had eight children together.

Ever the leader and visionary, Samuel W. Dexter created Washtenaw County's first newspaper, the *Western Immigrant,* in 1829. The next year, he plotted a village on the land around his home, calling it "Dexter" to honor his father. In the following years Mr. Dexter utilized his highly persuasive and influential voice to make it known that a railroad needed to be built through the community. When one came in 1841, it passed so close to his house (because the man donated some property for its construction) that Samuel soon had a mansion constructed outside the village of Dexter. The impressive domicile was called Gordon Hall, named after his mother, Catherine Gordon Dexter.

The architect of the grand estate house was Calvin T. Fillmore, brother of future U.S. president Millard Fillmore. As leading citizens, Samuel and Millicent Dexter hosted many high-society people, such as U.S. presidents James K. Polk and James Buchanan. It is probable but not known for sure that President Millard Fillmore also visited the mansion when he was in the region.

The Dexters were fierce abolitionists. Though not completely certain, historians surmise Gordon Hall served as a "station" on the Underground Railroad where runaway slaves would stop and rest for a couple of days while en route to freedom. Politically, Samuel W. Dexter was an Anti-Mason. Regarding the sale and consumption of alcohol, he was for temperance and gave a generous sum to the cause over time. In reference to the many stances the man took socially and politically, it was said of him: "[He] never consented to determine the moral elements of any question by the number of people who favored or opposed it."

Samuel W. Dexter lived at Gordon Hall until his death on February 6, 1863, aged 70. His many business activities were left to his son Wirt Dexter (born in 1831). Wirt sold most of the home's encircling land. On June 27, 1899, Samuel's wife, Millicent, the family matriarch, died. She was nearly 88 years old. Her will called for Gordon Hall to be sold, with the proceeds divvied up among her daughters. The historic structure was sold the next year, 1900, to another prominent citizen of Dexter.

The property passed through several hands, eventually falling into disrepair. In 1939 Katharine Dexter McCormick bought the estate. She was the granddaughter of Samuel and Millicent and the daughter of Wirt. Under her direction, Gordon Hall was restored to its earlier grandeur.

Katharine Dexter McCormick on April 22, 1913.

Katharine Dexter McCormick was born on August 27, 1875, in Dexter, Michigan, at her grandparents' mansion, Gordon Hall. She was raised in Chicago, where her father, Wirt, practiced law. However, after Wirt Dexter died unexpectedly of a heart attack at age 57, 14-year-old Katharine and her mother, Josephine, moved to Boston the next year, in 1890. Tragedy was common in the family— Katharine's brother Samuel died of meningitis four years later. He was only 25.

Katharine later graduated from the Massachusetts Institute of Technology (MIT) in 1904, obtaining a Bachelor of Science degree in biology. The same year, on September 15, the 29-year-old wed Stanley Robert McCormick, the youngest son of famed mechanical reaper inventor Cyrus McCormick. A year later the couple moved to Brookline, Massachusetts. The two never had children, and the marriage was forever marred by suffering because Stanley, very early on, slipped into severe mental illness. He was diagnosed with an affliction known today as schizophrenia and required hospitalization. Stanley's older sister, Mary Virginia, also suffered from the same disease of the mind. In 1909 the stricken fellow was declared legally incompetent. Katharine and the rest of the McCormick family were granted guardianship over him.

Mrs. McCormick, from an early age, was a strong advocate for advancing the rights of women. In 1909 she became vice president and treasurer of the National American Woman Suffrage Association and paid for the group's publication, *Women's Journal*. McCormick organized much of Carrie Chapman Catt's push to achieve ratification of the 19th Amendment to the U.S. Constitution, granting women the right to vote nationwide. In 1920, after the 19th Amendment was ratified, McCormick became vice-president of the League of Women Voters.

Through Catt, in 1917 McCormick met Margaret Sanger, the controversial birth control advocate. Katharine joined the cause. She worked with Sanger for decades. Over several years in the 1920s, McCormick smuggled over a thousand diaphragms from her estate in Europe (Geneva, Switzerland) to New York City and on to Sanger's Clinical Research Bureau.

Ever conscientious of her husband's abysmal condition, McCormick turned to the science of endocrinology to assist Stanley. Katharine had come to believe that a problem with an adrenal gland was what caused schizophrenia. To find a cure for the dreadful ailment, she established the Neuroendocrine Research Foundation from 1927 to 1947 at Harvard Medical School and subsidized the publication of the journal *Endocrinology*. This institution was the first to conduct studies on the connection between the endocrine system and mental illness.

Katharine Dexter McCormick's deep financial resources allowed her the means to endow or assist many charities, with one example being her creation of a research institution for the care of the mentally ill at Worcester State Hospital.

When Mrs. McCormick's mother, Josephine, died in 1937, aged 91, Katharine was left with an estate worth more than $10 million. Ten years later, in January of 1947, her husband, Stanley, passed away. He was 72. His death left Katharine with an initial amount of funds exceeding $35 million. However, it took five years to settle his estate—of which 85 percent went to the government via an inheritance tax.

In 1953 Katharine was introduced to Gregory Goodwin Pincus via Margaret Sanger. Pincus had been working on creating a hormonal birth control method since 1951 at his own research lab, the Worcester Foundation for Experimental Biology. The drug company that backed him quit funding his pioneering research because his efforts did not produce a profit. So McCormick picked up the slack and donated $2 million to him over the years until her death in 1967. This money is credited for bringing about the eventual successful development of an oral contraceptive pill. The U.S. Food and Drug Administration approved the sale of this pill in 1957 for menstrual disorders, and for contraception in 1960.

After this McCormick turned her attention to helping female students at her alma mater, MIT. She helped provide them with adequate housing, in part by donating a handsome sum of money to establish Stanley McCormick Hall, an all-female dormitory allowing the university to house 200 women students.

The philanthropist was active in supporting the arts too, her overall contributions being too many to list here. Katharine Dexter McCormick died at age 92 on December 28, 1967, in Boston, Massachusetts. The woman willed $5 million to the Stanford University School of Medicine to assist female physicians, $5 million to Planned Parenthood of America which funded the Katharine Dexter McCormick Library in New York City, and $1 million to the Worcester Foundation for Experimental Biology, among other gifts.

Chapter 2

Dreadful Hunts/Hold Your Fire

Milo Clark came to the town of Bronson in Branch County, Michigan, when just a lad of 14, arriving on Christmas Day, 1835. Along with his parents, Milo had come with a younger brother, Leonard, and three sisters (names not given). The family had been living in Norwalk, Huron County, Ohio. Jabez Clark, the family patriarch, had come to Ohio from Connecticut in 1816.

With the lone exception of young Milo, the family experienced much sickness throughout the year of 1836 while homesteading in their new surroundings of territorial Michigan. Due to their sufferings, a decision was made to head back to the family's unsold Ohio residence for a year before returning to Bronson in 1837.

When the Clarks first set foot in Bronson at the end of 1835, it was a tiny settlement of only eight houses. Upon the family's return Milo worked incredibly hard, and as a young man persevered, eventually becoming prosperous in business. Clark's main venture was to supply hardware to the local populace of the growing community. Living was tough but rewarding. However, life could have taken a different path for Mr. Clark—much different.

One day while hunting in the town's nearby wilds with a fellow named Sellers (full name unknown), Milo found himself in a harrowing, indeed dangerous, situation. The men, in their dogged pursuit of game, became separated—though not by far. While apart, a suspicious noise caught Clark's attention. Alarmed, the man leveled his firearm and pointed it in the direction the sound had come from. He saw no animal or person. However, very soon another noise made its way to the ears of the tense hunter, spooking him to no small degree. It was the snapping of a large twig or stick. Glancing around nervously, Clark spotted a panther about 40 yards distant. Although an exceptional marksman, Milo held his fire, considering his circumstances too risky. Instead of shooting at the panther, the hunter walked along cautiously, never once taking his eyes off the beast.

Soon Clark found himself in a clearing. The panther, which had also been watching his actions, then sped off further into the forest, "uttering angry screams." The retreat of the panther brought much relief to the man who had engaged in a very chilling but un-panicked restraint.

Hunter companion Sellers, on the other hand, who also glimpsed the large feline and heard its awful screech, nearly lost his "senses," running the entire way to "Holmes' mill," where he informed all folk around that a panther was after Clark.

A valid question emerges from this exciting account (no date given by the historical source, but likely in the 1850s). Why did Milo Clark, a man reputed to have an excellent shot, not take aim at the cougar and pull the trigger? Other hunters, experienced or novice, undoubtedly would have. Had Clark only a musket with a single loaded ball? Whatever the case, a cooler head prevailed as the man considered it a major risk to shoot under the conditions. Why? A wounded predator quite often attacks in a most enraged and ferocious manner, becoming much more dangerous than it otherwise would be.

Take the case of Kentucky farmer Richard Holt, killed and partially consumed by a panther some years later (1874) in Spencer County, Kentucky, near Taylorsville. Holt was out hunting, accompanied by a little boy (name unknown). The two caught sight of a panther walking nearby. Holt aimed and fired his gun two times at the beast, striking the animal's side, but "without fatal effects."

Within seconds the infuriated massive cat "landed upon Holt and was savagely clawing him to death." The young boy ran as fast as he could to a field about a half-mile distant, where a group of men were laboring. After hearing the kid's shrieking news of the big cat attack on the hunter, the men wasted little time in arming themselves and "hastened to Holt's assistance."

The rescue party arrived at the scene of the violent encounter much too late, however. The farm workers found what remained of the hunter, his "body torn almost into shreds." A portion of the recently deceased man's carcass had already been eaten, "as large lumps of flesh which had been torn out of the body could not be found anywhere about the spot." What about Richard Holt's assailant? The panther's whereabouts were completely unknown.

The dead fellow, Mr. Holt, was described as being quite fond of hunting, "brave to a fault," and "very venturesome." Right after the man's gruesome demise, many of the locals organized a major hunt to exterminate "the monster of the woods," whose "hideous yells" were said to be "heard every night." However, the nighttime slinkings of the wounded cougar went unchallenged, as "the people are afraid to pursue in the dark," wrote the *Louisville Ledger*.

The fate of the wounded big cat responsible for killing farmer Holt forever remains a mystery. Did the creature sooner or later succumb to its gunshot injuries, or did it make a substantial recovery, thus left able to live out a relatively healthy, normal life?

🐾

A letter printed in the *Minneapolis (Minnesota) Journal* from October 1896 describes a frightening encounter a hunter had with a panther in the forests of northern Wisconsin. John Henderson lived on a claim in the wilderness seven miles from the tiny community of Maple, Wisconsin, which was located around a train station along the Northern Pacific Railroad. The fellow and an acquaintance were out hunting partridge, or whatever else they could bag, in a dense pine forest. Henderson was about 200 feet in front of his partner when a "piercing shriek" split the air. The sound resembled "a woman in distress."

The disturbing cry had come from a very close distance, paralyzing the lead hunter with fear. After standing totally still for a few minutes, the man regained his wits enough to realize a panther was slinking about—one that many local persons had heard numerous times over the past couple of years but had never seen.

Mr. Henderson fearfully, but cautiously, started retracing his steps, his eyes scanning the surrounding trees. Turning around and gazing upward, he immediately caught sight of the big cat. Though armed, Henderson felt completely helpless as terror seemed to immobilize every nerve in his body.

The cougar crouched on a large tree branch with its big front paws fastened to a smaller limb. The animal appeared ready to make a spring at the frozen Henderson. Man and beast locked eyes on each other for about five minutes, neither one making the slightest move. However, in every second of the passing moments, the hunter expected the feline to leap at him.

Mr. Henderson wanted to shoot at the panther, but later admitted that he was so immobilized from fear he could not raise his firearm, nor turn and run. Finally a "rustling" was heard from nearby. The welcome sound was the result of the other hunter approaching his petrified companion. The cat, upon spotting the second man, let out another shriek and leaped from its position just over the head of Henderson. The creature landed on earth and tore off into the forest. Both men had zero interest in pursuing the beast.

While recovering from the shock the scary ordeal had given him, John Henderson felt a growing pain on the back of his left hand. A nasty scratch presented itself. The claws of one of the panther's paws had scraped him as the animal flew above. Evidently, the man had thrown up his left arm over his head in an instinctual defensive move, thus sustaining the wound. He was lucky. Maybe the cat was too. If the big cat had not fled it might have been killed in mortal combat with the two frightened but well-armed fellows. One will never know.

This dramatic episode took place roughly 30 miles due west of the town of Ironwood, Michigan, which sits on the far western Upper Peninsula border with Wisconsin. The specific big cat, unbeknownst to itself, likely spent its whole life among the northern wilderness of both states.

Chapter 3

Into Our Dwellings

The number of wolves and other wild animals which abounded in the forests was something remarkable. A venture into the darkness of the night was almost certain to be rewarded with the sight of one wolf or more, and occasionally a more savage animal made his appearance, to the terror of the settlers.

—Franklin Ellis, writing on the history of Fenton Township, Genesee County, Michigan

One night Mr. Alonzo J. Chapin, one of the original pioneers of Fenton Township, Genesee County, Michigan, was startled when his small dog began barking excitedly. The weather was warm, and on such nights the cabin door was often left open with a smudge outside to keep the mosquitoes at bay. But on this particular evening, due to rain, the door was kept shut.

Curious to discover what his canine continued to bark at, Mr. Chapin stepped out (unclad), glancing into the dark. The fellow quickly noticed a large animal which he surmised was a big dog. To frighten it away, Chapin threw several stones at the creature.

However, whatever the thing was, it stood its ground and just snapped at the projectiles.

Now very much alarmed, Alonzo Chapin "made a quick spring inside the house," slammed the door, "and placed his back against it." Immediately there was a massive thud against the outside of the door. The crash was of such force that it nearly knocked Chapin down. The terrified man figured the door would be smashed in, "despite his efforts to prevent it." The mysterious large animal, however, soon gave up its intent to gain entry inside the cabin and slunk away into the forest.

Shortly after Alonzo Chapin's narrow escape from the unknown beast, he and a man named Perry Lamb and another settler (name unknown) remained the only men in the new settlement (later known as the Cheney Neighborhood) healthy enough to help those in the vicinity who were plagued by serious illness. The good Samaritans traveled established routes among the log cabins of their neighbors to access them and provide assistance.

Close by Silver Lake dwelled a man, Harrison Tupper, and his brother, who lived next door. Alonzo Chapin paid a visit to Mr. Harrison Tupper, who was ill and bedridden. At the time, the ailing man's wife was outside the log home, milking cows.

While inside the dwelling a most unusual event took place. The head of the sick man's bed was positioned next to an open window. As Chapin sat in the room where Tupper lay, he witnessed the curtain of the open window begin to move. In the next instant, a massive paw entered through, pushing the curtain to one side. Then, "a savage-looking head" emerged, "and moved close to the face of the sick man." Chapin screamed out, grabbed his chair with both hands, and advanced toward the beast. The animal vanished.

In a couple of moments Mrs. Tupper came inside from her milking. Alonzo Chapin inquired of the woman if she knew who owned the large dog wandering about. She replied that she did not, but had seen the animal in the darkness while outdoors on several recent occasions.

Mr. Chapin then stepped outside the cabin to investigate, and soon after witnessed the creature leap onto the roof of the house of Harrison Tupper's brother just a few yards away. Chapin fired a stone at it, which caused the big critter to jump off the building and disappear into the wild. The sight of the fleeing beast witnessed by Chapin revealed the animal to be a panther.

During the following week the big cat was shot at several times by local citizens. Feeling threatened, the panther relocated southward into Springfield Township, Oakland County, where it was eventually slain—"and the settlement rid of a dangerous intruder." Undoubtedly to the unfortunate cougar, the real dangerous intruders were the recently arrived animals which walked upright on two legs.

However, to say persons who kill panthers are always in the wrong would be misguided, if not outright dishonest. These powerful and occasionally dangerous creatures sometimes enter the domiciles of humans, and therefore do pose a threat to both people and their domesticated animals. Consider the following other historic incidents.

One morning in mid- to late September of 1875, a husband and wife residing approximately nine miles east of Willis, Texas, departed from their home to engage in business. The two left their eldest child, a 12-year-old girl, in charge of the household.

Near noon the young lady heard her infant sibling (gender not given), 14 months old, who had been asleep on a bed in the adjacent room, emit a horrendous screech. Big sister, protector of the home, scrambled to see what was wrong. Upon opening the room's door, she witnessed a large panther leap over the bed and jump out an open window, all the while grasping the little child in its mouth. The older sister quite literally sprang into action by jumping onto the bed and then leaping out the same window the big cat had both entered and fled by.

Big sister's piercing screams brought forth her other siblings from the house to pursue the absconding beast. The family of children chased the panther quite a way to a barred fence which separated the property clearing from the forest. While being chased, the big cat dropped the baby but immediately scooped the child back up.

At the property line, the 12-year-old girl, determined to save her little sibling, bravely advanced to about 15 or 20 feet of the menacing feline. Her courage prevailed. The cougar let go of the little child, turned around, hurdled the fence, and took to the woods.

Older sister immediately grabbed up her youngest sibling and sped to the house. The rescued baby had been nearly asphyxiated from accumulated grass and sand which had filled its nose and eyes as the cat moved with the child through the yard. Fortunately, the little one soon recovered from the near-deadly experience, suffering only a few scratches and blood blisters from the cougar's fangs. The news account of the dramatic incident concluded with the unknown writer stating: "Too much praise cannot be bestowed on the brave girl who saved the child's life."

Another panther home invasion took place in the Lone Star State a few years earlier. The *Brenham (Texas) Banner* told of an account that occurred approximately mid-March 1872 whereby a cougar entered a house near Fort Griffin, Texas, and snatched up a child who had been sitting on the floor. The cat immediately sought to carry away its live human prey. Luckily, two men not far distant heard sounds of distress and successfully came to the child's rescue. The kid (age and sex unreported) was not seriously harmed.

What became of the big cat remained unknown to any reader of the small article. Few details were provided in the story. A follow-up report of the incident could not be found. However, similar accounts of such an event suggest the offending animal was soon tracked down by concerned citizens and dispatched. We will never know.

The *Yazoo (Mississippi) Register* from May 18, 1837, informed of a very dangerous and highly unusual panther encounter that had just taken place. A keel boat crew, after traveling upstream on the Yazoo River in the state of Mississippi, put in for the night on shore. At about 9 p.m. as the men were seated in a cabin, a big panther "sprung in at the door," and seized one of the fellows by the shoulder. The other three crew members rushed the cat and tried to pry their mate from the powerful jaws "of the monster," but to no avail.

One of the rescuers grabbed a long gun, aimed at the beast, and pulled the trigger. He missed his target in the blur of pulling, twisting, and thrashing action. The same man then quickly grabbed a Bowie knife and jammed the massive blade into the panther's heart; within moments the ferocious feline was dead.

The victim of the big cat's horrible attack was severely injured, "his shoulder nearly torn off, and his body lacerated by the claws of the infuriated monster," wrote the *Yazoo Register*.

The sheer level of gall and violence displayed by this particular cougar's aggression (attacking when four men were congregated together *and* while inside a dwelling) begs a couple of questions. Was what happened a so-called "hunger attack," wherein the big cat was so incredibly famished it resorted to extraordinary and highly risky measures to secure a meal? Or was the panther rabid and literally insane—due to having contracted the deadly rabies? These questions are pertinent—even though the answers will never be known. Finally, did the unfortunate boatman ever recover from his terrible wounds, or did he succumb to the awful injuries inflicted?

My research uncovered another long-ago incident of a panther entering the home of people, and as usual, the event didn't end well for the cat. The old Florida newspaper *Peninsula* mentioned an account from late November or early December 1869. Mr. Eli P. Whidden was inside his apparently open "dwelling" located in Manatee County, Florida, when in stalked a panther which jumped on his little daughter.

Whidden ran at the animal to save his child, causing the cat to release its small human quarry. The panther then turned its aggression to the father, bounding toward him. Whidden fled out of his domicile into the yard. The creature chased the terror-filled man around the outside of the house. Whidden grabbed a broadax and swung it at the beast, but the ax head came loose, flying off of the handle.

Retreating again, the frightened man did not give up. He gripped a foot-adze (an ax-like tool with a curved blade at right angles to the handle; used for shaping wood) and "laid his enemy dead at his feet." As is nearly always the case regarding old news coverage of such events, details of the occurrence were scant. Was the young girl seriously injured? How large was the panther? Was the predator male or female?

Like the long-ago past, the panther, cougar, puma, mountain lion, etc., still does on occasion make its way into the dwellings of humans. Today's difference is that when the encounters are reported, far more information is given. The outcome for the cat, though, is usually the same—the beast is laid low.

The gravestones of Genesee County, Michigan, pioneers Alonzo Chapin (July 31, 1812–January 11, 1884) and Elizabeth "Eliza" Gale Chapin (September 22, 1820–January 11, 1901). Husband and wife endured innumerable hardships during their early years of settlement, including Alonzo's very dangerous encounters with a panther of the wild. *Photos from www.findagrave.com*

PART II
THE LUMBERMAN'S PERIL

The Menace of the Manistee

Laboring in the lumber industry within Michigan's vast pine forests of yesteryear was highly dangerous work. There were numerous ways in which a man of the trade could be severely injured or killed due to the extremely difficult jobs that needed to be done.

Lumberjacks or "shanty boys," as the men were often called, were sometimes crushed to death by falling trees or from rolling logs when loading and unloading horse-drawn bobsleds. Arms, legs, hands, or feet were regularly mauled by errant ax swings or sliced horribly by crosscut saws. Those operating the large circular saws at sawmills were at times cut in half or had limbs severed completely—or at least had them mangled badly enough so as to require amputation.

Spike-booted rivermen, or "river hogs," had the most perilous occupation of the business. These fellows bore the responsibility of getting cut logs, usually 16 feet in length, downstream to the mills. With near-impeccable balance, the men, while utilizing their long, pointed, hooked poles, literally rode the massive logs downriver. Falling into the cold, rushing water happened frequently, as rivermen regularly lost their footing when swift-moving logs rammed each other. An unfortunate man could then easily be smashed between the butt ends of the huge sections of tree trunk. Or perhaps a river hog drowned from being knocked unconscious while in the river, or from having too many logs flow over his head, thus denying the ability to resurface.

Threats to the lumberman never abated. However, continuous risks to life or limb occasionally had nothing to do with the many different and dangerous tasks within the timber trade itself, but rather manifested from external forces having everything to do with the wider work environment—the great outdoors.

Chapter 4

A Treacherous Trek for Spring Water

A reporter for the newspaper *Isabella County Enterprise* (Mount Pleasant, Michigan), or perhaps the editor himself, wrote that he'd gotten wind of a 15-year-old boy being "torn up" by a panther at a (lumber) camp two miles out of Farwell, Michigan, in the Lower Peninsula. The alleged attack apparently occurred sometime during the first couple of weeks in August 1878 since the paper in which the event was reported is dated August 14, 1878.

Unnamed in the short article, the lad had been sent to fetch a bucket of water from a nearby natural, free-flowing spring. Soon after the young man left the logging area, his yells permeated the air. However, those who heard them paid the boy no heed because he was frequently "singing and hallooing."

After a while, taking note the teen had not returned, another lumberjack was sent for the water. There at the spring the unlucky youth was found lying in the dirt—having been torn "to pieces," stated the paper. It quickly became evident to those who investigated the scene that a panther had sprung upon the young worker's back as he leaned over to scoop up the water.

Very little is known about this particular tragedy, as a follow-up article could not be found. Nor could a death record matching a young male of the approximate age from Clare County, Michigan, where and roughly when the vicious attack apparently occurred.

A couple of possibilities may explain the dearth of information regarding this event. First, perhaps the young man did not die from the big cat attack, despite being "torn up" and badly mauled. Second, maybe the boy did die but not immediately. Gravely wounded, he may have been transported to a medical facility in another county where he, in time, succumbed to his wounds. These two guesses are plausible and would certainly explain the absence of a death record existing in the county (Clare) where the attack took place.

Another thought or two: If the youth did survive the horrific assault, the basic fact that he did not die would almost assuredly generate far less news than an actual killing by a wild beast, thereby explaining why such little reporting took place. And remember, official recordkeeping of all kinds was not as reliable so many years ago as during the modern era. Back then it was often sketchy at best. Therefore it is likely we will never know what the truth is regarding the terrible encounter.

Interestingly, only 17 months after the attack on the young lumberman near Farwell, the *Isabella County Enterprise* (January 7, 1880) reported yet another panther assault on a man. Even less information was provided than from the previous episode. A short blurb stated: "A man was attacked by an animal supposed to be a panther on the Bud[d] Lake railroad some days since."

Budd Lake exists near the center of Clare County, Michigan. The mid-Michigan town of Harrison borders it. I am not familiar with the history of the railway mentioned, but it was probably a short, narrow-gauge logging railroad typical in many areas of Michigan from about 1860 to 1900. Or else the rail line referred to in the newspaper was actually a trunk of the extensive Pere Marquette Railroad, which began to operate heavily throughout the region in that era.

Was the cat that allegedly attacked a man on the Budd Lake railway in late December 1879 or early January 1880 the same panther which tore apart the 15-year-old male near Farwell in early August of 1878? It certainly is possible since the events were less than a year-and-a-half apart, and locations of the attacks separated by no more than 15 miles (if connected by a straight line)—well within the home range of either an adult male or mature female cougar.

🐾

The *New Albany Democrat*, from September 16, 1847, in an ever-so-brief blurb account stated: "An Indian named Jo [ ] …living near Indian Lake, Hamilton County, N.Y. was recently torn to pieces by a panther."

Further investigation brought about greater details. As originally reported in the *Glenn Falls (New York) Clarion*, an Indian family living near Indian Lake, located in northern Hamilton County, state of New York, "recently numbered three male members." Fishermen and hunters of the region were well-acquainted with the trio of Native men, who were known as "Old Sable," "Lige," and "Little Jo."

According to the *Clarion*, Lige and Little Jo had recently spent the better part of a whole day tracking a panther. The brothers, however, could not locate the evasive animal. Dejected, the hunters retreated to their cabin for the night. In the morning, Little Jo woke early and walked to a nearby spring to slake his thirst from the cool, fresh, bubbling water flowing forth.

Either at the spring or close to it, a panther jumped the unsuspecting fellow and made quick work of him. The ferocious animal "literally tore" Jo "in pieces" before any help could arrive from the cabin, stated the *Clarion*.

The reader of the tragic account is left with several unanswered questions. For one, though it appears Little Jo was definitely killed, we do not know this for sure due to the exact wording in both news stories—neither of which actually said the victim of the attack died. However, Jo very likely, almost certainly, did meet death if he was indeed "torn to pieces."

Second, was the cougar which inflicted such devastation on Joe the same one he and his brother had pursued the day before? It is highly ironic if so. The hunter became the hunted.

A final question, common to these old accounts: What became of the man's assailant? Was the big cat soon afterwards tracked down by a party of men, perhaps with dogs, and dispatched? No follow-up stories were found. The true fates of both man and beast in this incident are forever lost in time.

In another case the *Logansport Journal* of Logansport, Indiana, printed a wired (telegraphed) account on August 26, 1854, of a child being slain by a panther near Clinch Mountain, in Washington County, Virginia. A woman, simply listed as a "Mrs. Bartlett," sent her little girl, exact name or age not mentioned, to a spring to obtain water. The chore being a common one, mother Bartlett became uneasy after her daughter did not return in the usual timeframe. So the woman went to search for her delinquent child, hoping to find the youngster sidetracked by some innocent curiosity.

Near the spring, Mrs. Bartlett was filled with dread upon sighting "traces of blood." Walking further, with a feeling of horror welling inside, the mother quickly and shockingly bore witness to "only a portion of the body of her child," proclaimed the *Journal*.

Not long after, having learned of the little girl's awful fate, many neighbors congregated together. Very near the spot where what was left of the innocent child was discovered, a big panther was spotted.

Unable to make an escape, the large cat was shot dead by members of the panther posse. The predator's sex and size were not given in the news dispatch—though those details would not have mattered to the family of the young victim, nor to the avenging villagers. Filled with sorrow, the locals were just relieved to rid their vicinity of a dangerous and deadly creature.

Perhaps natural springs within the wild are places where people need to be more cautious around than usual. Fauna of all kind, including predators of humans, probably frequent those spots more so than other areas which they inhabit due to the life-providing liquid spewing forth.

Are the three tragic long-ago cases from Michigan, New York, and Virginia—whereby humans met their end from the claws and fangs of wild panthers—just a matter of persons being in the wrong place at the wrong time, as is often the situation with any kind of victim? Or were their fates more probable, sealed in fact, because each location of death was actually more so a place of life, i.e., spring water?

Chapter 5

The Menace of the Manistee

In mid-January of 1882, a lumberman, specifically a "river hog" (those responsible for getting cut logs downriver to mills), was laboring at a logjam, i.e., "jam No. 2," located about 15 miles northeast of Manton, Michigan, on the Manistee River. The man, hard at work and therefore much preoccupied, did not hear or see the sneaking panther, which crouched close by.

Darkness was near. The workman carried a lantern and was in the process of crossing the river over a bunch of huge, entangled logs when, "without warning," the cat leaped upon him. Both of the worker's shoulders were dislocated from the "force of the blow." As he was being viciously torn, the desperate victim screamed for help. Fellow workers arrived in almost no time, but not quick enough. The poor man, mortally wounded, stayed alive long enough to inform his comrades that he had been attacked by a wild animal. Carried to camp by his would-be rescuers, the hapless soul succumbed to the terrible mauling within moments.

Newspaper accounts of the tragedy did not give the deceased man's name or age. Apparently the creature that was guilty of committing the assault was not tracked down and slain afterwards. A clean getaway was made. A writer for the *Elk Rapids Progress* of Elk Rapids, Michigan, had no doubt that a killer cat was responsible for the lumberman's death, writing: "The fact that a panther has before been seen along the Manistee and from the man's statement leads to the conclusion."

Some weeks after the fatal attack on the lumberman, the *Manton Tribune* reported in its February 7, 1882, edition that "a large panther was seen" the previous week by a man named Ezra Monroe. The sighting took place "between the village [of Manton] and Green's Mill." The news story continued: "His royal highness is about eight feet long and very fierce to look upon. This is perhaps the same one that killed the river-driver, mention of which was made several weeks ago … his favorite haunts are along the Manistee River and its tributaries. His beautiful voice has many times been heard by different settlers … it is hoped that his recklessness will be the cause of his downfall before he does further mischief."

Nearly a full year later, the *Presque Isle County Advance* out of Rogers City, Michigan, reported in an early January 1883 printing that a panther had been menacing a lumber camp near Grayling, Michigan. The *Advance* had gotten the article from its original source, the *Lumberman*, place of publication unknown—probably Crawford County, Michigan.

Though the piece was informative, its tone was somewhat jocular, if not critical. The author mocked the recent fear among local lumberjacks brought about by a wild panther seen and heard in the Grayling region. He belittled their fright by comparing the situation

to the tremendous difficulties that had befallen the nation's early settlers: "The hardy pioneers who first settled the country north and
west met with untold hardships and perils. … In those days men
went abroad and took their chances on what came, but such has been
the advance of civilization that a single panther in a section of pine
woods will scare the gall out of all the loggers in the district. Near a
camp in the vicinity of Grayling, Mich[.], one of these animals has
recently been several times seen and heard, its wild half human cry
falling with a chill on the ears of those who heard it."

The news story went on to mention how one of the camp's lumberjacks had a most unsettling experience with the "savage cat," as
he barely averted an attack. The worker was standing at the (river)
banking ground when he caught sight of the big cat "swiftly steal-
ing" toward him. When the fearsome creature stalked to a spot just
a few feet from the unarmed, terror-stricken man, "it crouched for
a spring, the swish of its tail sounding ominous." Just then, as if by
divine intervention, the cries of a bunch of approaching men rang
out. Before the oncomers reached the would-be panther prey, the
large feline had fled. As a result of the incident, the paper stated:
"The men have now become so thoroughly frightened that one of
them could not be hired to go away from camp after dark."

And justifiably so. The near-victim of a big cat attack had found
himself in a very perilous situation. The man probably would have
suffered a terrible mauling—possibly to the point he would've no
longer breathed life itself. If a cougar's claws don't kill its intended
prey, its jaws will—through strangulation or the breaking of neck
vertebrae.

But the Grayling area jacks were most likely already fearful; they
had to have been mindful of the (previously mentioned) deadly panther attack on the lumberman working the logjam not too far distant
and not quite yet a full year prior.

❧

The *Crawford Avalanche*, of Crawford County, Michigan, made brief mention in its August 16, 1894, edition of a not-so-distant local historical event (among others) in which a "big" panther was killed on the Manistee River near Grayling, Michigan, in 1883. When in 1883? The newspaper did not say. The only other information given was that it happened not far from a "Hanson's" (lumber) camp. Questions arise.

Was this slain panther the very same one that fatally mauled the laborer who was working at logjam No. 2 on the Manistee River, 15 miles northeast of Manton, Michigan, in mid- to late January of 1882? The scene of that particular attack is no more than about 20 miles southwest of Grayling—a short distance within either a male or female cougar range.

Was the dead cat the same one which readied itself for a spring upon the lone, terror-stricken lumberman at a riverbank near Grayling, Michigan, in late December 1882 or early January 1883? The river in this incident was not named by the news source. It could have been the mighty Au Sable River instead of the Manistee, as both major Michigan streams flow within a relatively short distance of each other at or near Grayling. So, whether both big cat–human encounters were on the Manistee or one on the Manistee and one on the Au Sable is irrelevant as to whether the same cat was responsible or not, because the two major waterways flow so closely together near Grayling.

Both incidents, one deadly, the other which very well could have ended fatally (regarding the man involved), beyond a doubt would have had local citizens—lumbermen especially—on the alert and lookout for such a beast. An untold number of people in the region were almost certain to be at the ready to shoot the big cat menace. And it may have happened, for at least one panther, according to the aforementioned news report, was done away with in the area shortly after the two occurrences.

Knowing this, the question is begged: Was this specific slain panther *the* cat—the Menace of the Manistee?

PART III
SUFFER THE LITTLE CHILDREN

A Gruesome Discovery

Apex predators of all types favor attacking the very young or old of the various large animals that make up their menu. The reason is simple and rather obvious—the immature and aged large prey animals put up far less of a fight than healthy adults of whatever the species. A greater resistance from the bigger, healthier animals of prey may spell doom for the predator if the right movements and tactics are utilized by the creature which has been set upon and attacked.

Big cats of every kind, along with bear species and large canines such as wolf and coyote, have all been kicked, stomped, trampled, or gored to death while attacking large prey. Or the predator was wounded so severely its ability to take future prey was tremendously compromised—to the point early death came via starvation or disease.

Predator animals instinctively know the danger of attempting to take the healthiest of given large prey, therefore they will tend to go after the young or old that are, if not smaller, definitely weaker and slower. So although some animal victims of apex predators are indeed full-grown, strong, and healthy, it is likely due to the fact that the very young or old of the species were, at the time, unavailable to be made into a meal.

We know the mountain lion, i.e., cougar or panther, is no different than other large carnivores—it can and often will successfully take a healthy, strong, full-grown bull elk in its prime and many times the cat's size. Or it will kill a whitetail or mule deer in the same category—mature and healthy. The same with a mountain goat or domesticated livestock such as horses, bovines, and pigs. Again, however, the Western Hemisphere's second largest cat (only the jaguar is larger), if it has its pick, will go after the very young or very old of its big prey fauna.

This includes humans. The cougar easily senses a baby or child is easier food to obtain than a fully grown healthy adult person—if the big cat is ever inclined to make such a move.

I made mention in my first book, *Swamp Rattler*, that all human death is sad. However, a caveat was stated saying that some human death is more tragic and grievous than others. And that would be the demise of children, whatever the cause. Kids of all ages who die young have barely begun to experience and enjoy life as grown-ups have, especially middle-aged and elderly adults. Children have a certain level of innocence that is more precious than that of mature persons. It is why there will always be a hierarchy within the realm of the deceased, with the death of children universally considered the most sorrowful.

With that understood, I urge the reader of this work to not be harsh when assessing the worthiness of the panther's existence. Do not be too judgmental against this particular carnivore for having slain human children on occasion. The incidents are few and continue to be highly rare when put into context. Perspective is needed when evaluating this wild creature of North, Central, and South America (the most widely distributed large mammal in all of the Western Hemisphere).

Of every unique animal species that exists, nature propels each one to do what it does. The cat is no exception. They are genetically programmed to act as they do. Therefore, the American panther is not morally culpable for preying on various creatures, humans included—even the little ones.

Chapter 6

A Blood-Curdling Tale

"**A** Blood-Curdling Tale," was reported by the *Crawford Avalanche*, on September 8, 1892, originating from the little town of Fergus, Saginaw County, Michigan. An absolutely horrific killing of a little child had just taken place.

In Saginaw County's Marion Township, a mother had left her young one (age, sex, and name not listed) asleep in a wagon while she picked blackberries not far away. The woman's first name was not provided, but her last name was reported to be "Greenbaum." Upon returning to the wagon, the woman made a sickening discovery: "A quantity of blood where her child had been," and the "mangled remains" of a single leg.

Investigators later speculated that "the child was devoured by a lynx or some wild animal of that species." This gruesome theory was bolstered by an eyewitness account from a married couple, Warren and Dora Mathewson of Fergus, who claimed to have seen "an animal resembling a panther" while also picking berries in the vicinity. "It is thought by some to be the same one that killed the child," the newspaper stated.

Mother Greenbaum was said to be so shaken and distraught, "fears are entertained that she will lose her reason," intoned the story's writer. The article ended by declaring that a search for "further traces" of the missing and obviously deceased child to be without positive result.

Questions abound regarding the terrible incident. One, where was the wagon's horse or horses during the time the child was under assault? The animal or animals would assuredly have made quite a ruckus or stir upon becoming aware of a major predator nearby. Perhaps they had been tethered to trees a good deal distant in order to graze and were therefore oblivious to the horror that was happening.

Second, how did the child's mother not physically hear the awful event as it was taking place—unless she was actually quite a ways away during the time? Maybe, in reality, a wild animal was never actually the culprit regarding the little one's demise. Could it be that what truly happened was an awful, tragic instance of child murder by parent, i.e., infanticide, carried out by an emotionally unhinged, deranged, or hopelessly depressed mother? If this was the case, blaming a child's death on a wild beast—bear, wolf, bobcat, or panther—would be rather convenient for the human perpetrator.

No other news story mentioning the mysterious and brutal death of the child could be found, nor could a Saginaw County death certificate be located for a little kid named Greenbaum (or other name) indicating such a horrific experience occurred that year (1892). However, if the story's details are indeed correct it is highly probable the innocent life of the sleeping child was taken by a hungry panther.

Though cougar numbers in Michigan had no doubt dwindled considerably by the 1890s due to the advance of civilization, the state's big cats were almost certainly still prowling the wilds of the

Lower Peninsula in that decade. And the killing of children by panthers was not unique to the Great Lakes State in the days of old.

🐾

In another case, an extremely sad story went out to Illinois newspapers from a correspondent of the *St. Louis Democrat* who reported that a little girl, name not given, 8 years of age, and a child of Mr. Joshua Taylor, who lived approximately 12 miles west of Jackson County, Illinois, was set upon by an unknown beast and killed. The tragedy occurred on Friday, July 17, 1863. The child had been sent alone by her parents on an errand to a neighbor's place. On her return trip the youngster was intercepted by some *thing* and never made it home.

Soon after, the girl was found lying lifeless not far from the road she had just strolled upon. Her body was by the side of a log and buried with leaves. The animal responsible for the 8-year-old's death was theorized to be a wildcat, a.k.a. bobcat, or a panther. One longtime citizen of Jackson County, a resident for 60 years, commented that this was the first instance he had ever known about of a human being slain by a wild creature in the county.

More information on the terrible event eluded this researcher, as a follow-up story was not located. So, more questions remain unanswered. For instance, was the offending animal ever tracked down and killed? Was the child-killer really a cat? The likely answer to the latter question is "yes" because the deceased's body was covered with leaves and other debris—weeds, grass, twigs—in typical feline fashion. Both bobcats and cougars cache the animals they've slain as a natural instinct to conceal a meal from other creatures so they may return later to resume their feast.

If the guilty animal in this case really was a cat, which kind was it? The answer is anyone's guess, since both critters—bobcat or panther—would easily be capable of carrying out a kill against a young, small person. But which species is more likely to have blood on their fangs in this instance? A panther for sure. Why? Because bobcat (or its close relative, the lynx) attacks on humans, be they children or grown-ups, are known to be exceedingly rare—quite rarer than attacks by cougars. The following story reveals another historical occurrence of panther predation on human children.

Way, way back in early July of 1870, a dispatch from the *Parkersburg Gazette* of West Virginia stated that 15 or 20 miles from Beverly, West Virginia, on the Middle Fork River, Randolph County, a "horrible affair" occurred in late June.

Two young boys—brothers—10 and 6 years of age, set out in the evening to drive home some cows. The kids were sons of Mr. Samuel Currence. Not far from their house, the youngsters were ambushed by a huge panther. The older boy quickly and courageously swept up his younger brother into his arms and attempted to make an escape.

The selfless and devoted act proved futile, however, as the giant cat's paws tore the younger boy from his older brother's grasp. Big brother, realizing another attempt at rescue of his sibling was impossible, sprinted for home. Soon father Samuel and the older son arrived at the scene of the attack, but discovered it was too late to save the younger boy. The ravaged remains of the doomed child were found "almost entirely devoured."

The newspaper account ended there, but the real story obviously continued even though a follow-up report could not be located—assuming there ever was one. So, additional facts of the tragedy are not known today and may never be brought to light.

We do not know as of this point, so many years later, if the offending beast was hunted down and killed afterwards. If so, was it a male or female? If shot dead, what was its weight and length (from nose tip to end of tail)?

Additional information linked to this particular tragedy is not likely to ever come forward after such an immense lapse of time (since 1870).

❧

The Bois Brule Bottom was a large floodplain region consisting of woods, swamp, and brush patches which lay between a range of hills where the town of St. Mary's, Missouri, is located and where the Mississippi River flows. For many weeks in May, June, and July of 1892, the bottom was covered with floodwater, making the area uninhabitable for both humans and fauna—including the occasional panther and wildcat, i.e., bobcat.

All animals normally dwelling in the Bois Brule Bottom were forced to take to the adjacent highlands, where people and their farms existed. This condition set the stage for an extremely tragic event whereby a baby's life was violently extinguished.

Mrs. Williamson, wife of a Henry Williamson, was working in the family's farmyard three miles south of St. Mary's on a Saturday morning in June of 1892. The woman's baby was lying down near her (either on a blanket in the yard or on the house porch). While focused on routine chores, Mrs. Williamson heard a strange sound behind her. She turned around just as a "huge panther" leaped a fence and landed in the yard.

Horror-stricken, the mother watched the beast grab her baby in its mouth, jump back over the fence and scamper off into the woods. The woman's shrill screams quickly brought an alarmed male neighbor to the yard from a hundred yards away. He was armed with a rifle. Both quickly took off in pursuit of the abductor and infant.

About a half-mile distant, the two caught up with the cat as it crouched in some bushes with the babe between its paws. The man fired his gun over the large predator to scare it into releasing the little one and run off. The panther let go of its quarry and retreated a short distance, allowing the dread-filled woman a chance to rush to her motionless child.

The mother's valiant effort to save her infant babe proved sadly in vain. The little one was lifeless, the cougar's teeth having punctured deep into the victim's neck. Death was likely instantaneous if the child suffered a snapped vertebra, and not much longer if from suffocation.

After a short span of time, "squads of men" took after the deadly cat and were able to successfully shoot it dead later in the afternoon of the same day the horrible attack occurred. The panther was slain about two miles from where it had been found with the dead child in its clutches.

Later that same year, south of Wichita, Kansas, at a place of commerce known as Hopkins' Trading Post located near a Cherokee reservation, an "Indian child" was killed by a panther. The horrible event occurred in plain view of the young one's mother. This happened in mid- to late November of 1892.

"The beast's cries had been heard for several nights, but none of the few inhabitants had the courage to attempt to kill it," wrote one newspaper.

Soon after the tragedy, "an old Indian scout," William Simmons (or possibly "Timmons") appeared on site. The courageous fellow successfully tracked the "brute" down and killed it close to the (Kansas-Oklahoma Territory) border. The big cat measured seven feet from its nose to tail tip. Whether the panther was a male or female was not mentioned in the news articles researched, nor was the sex and age of the victim child.

Eight years after the Native child was slain by the panther in Kansas, another big cat killing of kids occurred. This event was a double tragedy and took place in mid- to late November of 1900.

Jesus Luterio, a ranch hand living near Costulla, Texas, experienced the terrible loss of two of his children via separate attacks—almost certainly from the same animal. The little ones were aged 18 months and 2½ years. Neither of the young human prey's sex was provided by the news source.

The first victim, younger or older sibling not mentioned, was snatched away in the early morning after sunrise. A thorough search was conducted, but the child was not located. At the time numerous people were busy looking for the missing youngster, it was not yet known that a panther was the cause of the child's disappearance.

Some hours later, in the afternoon, the missing one's mother, to her horror, witnessed a cougar pounce upon and carry off her second child. Four men from the ranch with a team of tracking dogs launched a frantic search for the little child abductee and abducting feline. The canines eventually caught up with the fast-fleeing though highly exhausted cat. The men were trailing not far behind. However, before a single one of the human pursuers could reach the group of circling hounds, the panther had killed four of them.

The killer beast, though, like so often is the case when preying on a human or their prized livestock, essentially signed its own death warrant. For the big cat was instantly "laid low with a rifle," stated a newspaper. The grief-stricken mother of the two slain children was said to have gone "crazed" by the dreadful experience. Because of her indescribably horrific emotional state, she was transported to San Antonio for medical care.

The final two reports discovered through careful research, whereby children died by the claws or jaws of the American panther, are much briefer than the previous ones. The tragedies cry out for more delving, digging, and discovery by any persons interested in historical accounts of encounters between people and the big cat beast known by so many names—panther, puma, cougar, and mountain lion, among others.

A dispatch printed on December 1, 1894, in the *Thorntown Argus*, proclaimed that a baby had been carried off by a panther at "Jones's Mill," Oregon. The infant was afterward found "lifeless" in an adjacent forest. Save for a few scratches on the face, the victim's little body was not ravaged or mutilated.

Michigan's *South Haven Sentinel* stated in its August 22, 1896, edition that a panther killed two children, last name Allen, near Mansfield, Missouri. That was it. No more details were given.

This author hopes and desires that by at least a bare mentioning, others will be inspired to dig further into these occurrences in order to illuminate what the approximate, if not exact, truths are regarding them.

PART IV
THE BERRIEN COUNTY TERROR
AND OTHER ACCOUNTS

The Terror's End

Chapter 7

Gigantic Panther Slain

The most dreaded wild beast which, fortunately, was not so common, was the panther. These cats often grew to be eight feet or more from nose to tip of its long tail and they were powerful and dangerous animals. The cry of the panther was unlike that of any other animal, being like that of a wailing woman, and it was an eerie sound, sometimes late at night, after the candles had been put out, the fire in the fireplace banked for the night, and the folks had retired to the comforts of the feathered bed, to hear the wailing cry of a panther as it slunk around the little cabin in the wilderness.

—Ralph Ballard, writing in *Tales of Early Niles*
(Berrien County, Michigan)

October 13, 1857. On motion from Mr. Miller Resolved—That every person who shall kill a full grown panther in this county shall be entitled to a bounty of fifteen dollars subject to the provisions of Chapter fifty one of the compiled laws of Michigan—Adopted.

—Berrien Co. Board of Supervisors Minutes
(Berrien County, Michigan)

Berrien County, Michigan, contrary to historian Ralph Ballard's claim of panthers being not "so common," had long been a hot-bed region of human-panther encounters as evidenced by many old newspaper accounts. For example, the *St. Joseph Herald* of St. Joseph, Michigan, indicated in its January 23, 1875, printing that, "A reported panther in the woods south of Three Oaks is creating quite a sensation among the women and children of that vicinity."

Many more accounts came forth over the years, culminating in a particularly dramatic case. The *Newberry (Michigan) News*, on November 1, 1895, under the heading "Peninsular State News," reported from a dispatch that: "A wild animal, resembling a panther, is terrorizing farmers northeast of Niles [Michigan], and few venture out after night."

Indeed, for some years prior a mysterious beast, said to be a panther, had been driving fear into the hearts of locals in the extreme southwestern portion of Michigan's Lower Peninsula.

For a long time the creature went largely unseen, but was frequently heard, especially at night when people were in bed and its frightening cries rang out. Farmers, after hearing the beast's nocturnal screams, quite often later discovered numbers of their livestock dead or missing, having been slain and feasted on by the suspected cougar.

One man, William Goyette, had a close encounter with the Berrien County, Michigan, big cat, which afterwards left him considered to be incredibly fortunate by neighbors.

The *Alma (Michigan) Record*, of February 12, 1897, wrote: "Residents in the little hamlet of Brownstown, in Berrien County, stay close to their firesides after nightfall now."

Why? The newspaper explained that Mr. William Goyette came very close to being seriously mauled or killed by a big panther he had witnessed "trying to gain access" into his horse barn.

Upon spotting the hungry, foraging beast, the alarmed man

grabbed up a sizeable stone and chucked it at the unwelcome intruder. But the large cat quickly dodged the projectile. Angered by the whizzing rock, the panther hunkered down and quickly slunk toward Goyette. With no firearm, knife, or blunt instrument with which to defend himself, the fellow took to his heels and managed to safely dash into the family home.

A day or two later, an armed party of fellow Brownstown residents trailed the cat's tracks into the nearby hills. There the panther's pursuers stumbled upon the carcass of a horse, half-devoured. The unfortunate animal had not long before strayed too far from the safety of its farm quarters.

The panther posse's tracking soon ended—stymied—unable to successfully hunt down the terror of Berrien County. However, the panther's days were numbered with each new affront to civilization.

🐾

"Gigantic Panther Slain," was the title of the original article, and its wired dispatches, to newspapers throughout Michigan—in fact the entire Midwestern United States—appearing in late November of 1899. The subheading of the title was even more dramatic. It read: "Beast That Has Terrorized Michigan Farmers for Years Has Finally Been Slain."

The news account stated that for 10 years, farmers living near the "wild hills," 12 miles south of St. Joseph, Michigan, had been plagued by an "immense" panther which frequently decimated their flocks.

But apparently critters on four legs were not the only creatures to fall prey to the cougar. The ferocious cat was believed by the locals to have killed and eaten a man, John Croll, who completely vanished when traveling through the hills some years earlier. The man's whereabouts continued to remain a mystery, but many in the area suspected he suffered a horrible fate—from the fangs and claws of the notorious beast.

Whether the panther took the life and made a meal of Mr. Croll or not, the cat's reign of terror soon came to an abrupt end. In November of 1899, James Woodward, while hunting at the edge of the hills, caught a glimpse of the notorious big cat feasting on a calf it had just killed and either dragged or carried off from an adjoining pasture.

Quietly and cautiously Mr. Woodward snuck close to the crouched predator as it preoccupied itself with its most recent meal. After "slipping an extra cartridge of bullets into his gun," the man's aim proved true. The Berrien County Terror's life was extinguished by a single trigger pull.

A short while later the dead predator's body was hauled off to the little town of Bridgeman, two miles away. Temporarily put on display, the carcass of the legendary big cat created a heap of "excitement" among townsfolk.

How could such a brazen beast exist for as long as it did, after doing what it did to the local livestock, and perhaps to a wandering man as well? The writer of the big cat's demise offered up an explanation: The fact that the trees and shrubs atop the hilly terrain of the region had grown unmolested for the previous 50 years made the area extremely dense and thus difficult for humans to penetrate. The place, therefore, had become perfect for wild creatures to dwell and remain undetected, if not impossible to find.

But even the thick cover was not enough to continually protect the ravaging creature. It obviously made one too many forays into (or at least close enough to) civilization—as the hunter Woodward's bullet demonstrated.

The dramatic documentation of the Berrien County Terror's death came up short, as the stories of the day almost always did, e.g., was the slain panther a male or female? It would be interesting to know. What did the creature weigh? How long did the beast measure, from nose tip to tail tip? The relevant answers, like so many others, have been lost through the passage of time.

Chapter 8

The Panther's Den

It was the summer of 1860, July 4th or Independence Day to be exact, when a fellow left his precious wife and babe behind and began a very long sojourn on foot, heading from the early Grand Traverse settlement in Michigan's northwest Lower Peninsula to Kalamazoo, Michigan, far to the south.

Delbert Ivins was young and hardy, so he planned on making the great distance in good time. He traveled light and walked with a steady gait upon the old "Traverse Trail." At about five miles south of Pine River and 30 miles south from his place of departure, the strong but tiring man was thrilled to discover a bubbling brook trickling over the well-worn pathway. It flowed from a nearby spring. The fresh water would quench the traveler's thirst and cool his sweaty brow.

While taking a much-needed and well-deserved break the man discovered a little log hut, covered in bark, a few yards up the little stream. The structure was likely the winter quarters of some hunter or trapper, figured Ivins. It was relatively clean and tidy inside.

The location of the refreshing spring and tiny cabin was about 15 miles short of a settlement where the sojourner had hoped to stop and rest for the night. However, it was already late in the day, nearing sundown in fact, so Mr. Ivins decided he'd stay put and camp at the convenient location overnight. The fellow gathered up some dried leaves, sticks, and small, dead tree limbs to set ablaze within the fireplace in the center of the dwelling. The fire's purpose was not so much for warmth during the night as it was to "smoke away" the multitude of mosquitoes swarming through the door-less, open hut. Hemlock boughs were placed in a back corner of the little domicile to serve as bedding for the man.

Upon settling down within the cabin, Ivins lit his pipe and opened a folded newspaper cutout he had brought with him. He tried to read, but could not concentrate as a growing uneasiness took hold of his mind. The traveler soon heard what he thought was human whispering. It called his name, then admonished him to leave, for the cabin was haunted. In disbelief, Ivins's frightened eyes darted all around the little structure, attempting to discover the source of the soft, chilling voice. His vision caught nothing.

The spooked man then stepped outside the hut to look around but spotted no person about—only the setting sun, which resembled a massive fireball. Birds of the forest happily chirped away, but the growing breeze sounded lonesome and dreary blowing through the tall pines and hemlock trees surrounding the cabin. The evening was warm, but the man felt frigid. He pondered his situation for a few moments, then concluded it was time to leave the place. Ivins quickly packed his few belongings, grabbed his "carpet-sack," and started off for the settlement he had initially wished to reach.

However, no sooner than he had reached the trail, the man stopped to rethink what he was doing. Considering it was growing extremely dark and 15 miles a long way to travel in those particular hours of night, Ivins determined there was a real possibility of wandering off the trail and getting hopelessly lost. So the fellow changed his mind, deciding to "risk the phantoms and stay."

Feeling calmer now, the traveler returned to his place of shelter, as frightening as it had been. He collected more fuel for the flames on his way. Once inside, Ivins sat down to relax, relit his pipe, and again pulled out the piece of newspaper to read. But he still could not focus enough to comprehend the printed words. After sitting for an hour and occasionally feeding the fire, Ivins retreated to his makeshift bed of soft hemlock. He prayed to be overtaken by a sound and peaceful slumber. Sleep did not come instantly, but in about a half-hour the fellow dozed off and finally felt the comfort he so desperately desired.

However, the weary man's comfortable rest was not to continue. A "fearful scream" jolted the fellow awake. Ivins, startled, quickly threw more sticks and branches onto the fire, which had nearly burned out. The flames rose and brightened the inside of the little structure once more. Now standing, Ivins in "breathless silence" strove "to catch the slightest sound," but only detected the wind continuing to blow through the branches of the tall pines and hemlock at varying speeds.

In a minute, however, another terrible sound pierced the darkness. It was not the same as the one which had awakened him, but was so "frightful and unearthly," Ivins later wrote, "that I fairly sank down paralyzed with fear!"

More dreadful noises rang out—"snarlings, growlings, and gnashing of teeth, commingled with yells, groans, bellows of pain, terror and despair."

Delbert Ivins was no stranger to the deep forest, having hunted and trapped game on numerous occasions while also camping out many a night—far, far from the comfortable confines of civilization.

But the man had never, ever heard the shockingly disturbing noises he was now confronted with.

Compounding the man's terror was the knowledge he possessed no firearm. His only protection came in the form of a "stout" cane and pretty good pocketknife. So Ivins resolved that if he was to be killed by the (still unknown) beast of the woods, it would not be without a grand fight on his part.

The sojourner bravely walked to the open doorway, readying himself with open knife in one hand, cane in the other. He peered outward. As he scanned his surroundings, a thought entered his brain: Maybe some hunters had come up to the cabin, saw it to be presently occupied, and therefore decided to play a trick or joke on the unsuspecting lone dweller—himself.

Ivins therefore called out to the possible jokesters, imploring them to make themselves known to him. The fear-stricken fellow even invited them to join him, giving assurance that they'd be for-given for the prank and treated with courtesy. But before he even finished yelling out the statement, the would-be host eyed something in the distance "creeping" his way. When within 50 feet, whatever it was let loose another "round" of the same hellish-sounding barrage it had emitted moments earlier.

As the creature slowly but steadily slunk forward, Ivins, to his horror, glimpsed that the source of the wretched noises was not a man or men playing a game, but indeed a wild panther. Feeling desperate, the man seized the unburned end of one of the torched branches within his fire and flung it at the approaching cat as hard as he could. He missed his target. The big feline merely growled as it retreated into a thicket. But the beast only disappeared for a brief period.

Soon the panther re-emerged and began a vigil, one that would last several hours. The menacing animal circled the small cabin at least a half-dozen times throughout the night, while often stopping a few feet in front of the open doorway to peer inside at its fear-stricken occupant. Whenever the fire inside burned lower, the large cat became more emboldened, slinking closer to the door opening, issuing threatening growls. The captive man, in return, would speak out loudly to the panther, as if lecturing the beast, in an effort to prove he was not the least bit afraid. By doing so Ivins hoped to lessen the cat's aggressive actions. But inside his skin, if not on the outside, the fellow was trembling.

The besieged traveler could have kicked himself for not bringing his long gun or pistol as means of protection during the lengthy journey. About two hours before daylight, Ivins's fuel supply within the tiny cabin had diminished considerably, practically inviting the big cat to dash in. It would not be very long before the leaves, sticks, and branches would be used up. The cornered man envisioned himself being torn to pieces and eaten by the panther. He wondered what would become of his wife and baby without himself in their lives.

In an instant, despair gave way to panic; Ivins wildly scraped up and threw into the waning fire the sole remaining leaves, wood chips, sticks, and small, broken tree branches. The flare-up of the flames was brief, as the fire quickly died down once again. The desperate fellow glanced at the doorway and saw that the panther was now at the very entrance itself, rather than hovering some feet back, "his eyes glaring like two balls of fire, while he growled ferociously!"

With death literally at the doorstep, Ivins hit upon an idea not thought of before and began rapidly tearing at—and pulling down—the loose bark above him which served as both the hut's ceiling and roof. Tossing the dried chunks of Mother Nature into the embers, the fellow soon had the fire roaring. The panther backed away from the door a few feet and stayed put until morning began its approach.

Light soon appeared in the eastern sky. Dawn was soon to break. As it got lighter with each passing moment, the big cat let out a series of "heart-rendering, hair-raising" screeches, turned eastward, and walked off. In a couple of minutes, the terrifying creature was no longer seen nor heard.

Not long after the panther's exit, Ivins gathered his few possessions and departed the hut. For the first few miles of his resumed journey, he kept a rapid pace. Near the end of his second day of travel, right before the sun once again set, Ivins reached his destination—the "Dry Prairie Settlement," 55 miles from the tiny cabin the fortunate man would forever after refer to as the "Panther's Den."

The night with the big cat had been the absolute worst one of his entire existence, wrote Delbert Ivins 30 years later. However, surviving the frightful, life-threatening encounter had instilled in the young man a powerful sense of gratitude and appreciation for life—a feeling which forever remained, never to drift away.

Chapter 9

The Beast of Brighton

The *South Lyon Pickett* of South Lyon, Michigan, ran a short article in mid- to late December 1886 about a panther attack on two men which occurred a week or two earlier on a Saturday near Brighton, Michigan, in Livingston County.

While traveling through the woods two miles east of Brighton, a couple of fellows—Nelson Gould and Charles Meach—stumbled upon a "beast of the lynx species," as the creature was devouring an (animal) carcass. The protective cat gave the men "no chance to get out of the way," and sprang at them.

Mr. Gould was armed with a revolver and shot the large beast, breaking one of its hind legs. Seemingly unaffected, the animal, utilizing its three good legs, jumped upon the man and immediately grabbed one of his arms in its mouth, "tearing the flesh from Gould's arm," and shredding his clothes "into rags."

Meanwhile, Charles Meach, armed with an ax, "struck fiercely" at the attacking cat. One of his swings struck the animal's skull, killing it instantly. However, Gould had already shot the large cat "three times while fighting, but [with] none of the shots seeming to take effect," the news report stated.

The dead "brute" was soon weighed, showing it to be 87 pounds and declared to be a "genuine panther." The sex of the big cat was not given. It could have been a young male near adulthood or a grown female. Mature male cougars weigh between 110 and 200 pounds while adult females range from about 75 to 120 pounds on average.

After the dramatic event, there was speculation that the deceased big cat had escaped from a (circus) menagerie, "as nothing of the kind has ever been seen about Brighton before," the newspaper claimed.

While it is theoretically possible the panther could have escaped detention by humans, the more likely scenario is that the beast was wild and from a remnant (albeit shrinking) native Michigan population. With the advance of civilization over the passage of time, i.e., the clearing of forests, drainage of swamps, establishment of farms, building of cities, and construction of major roads, etc., many news personnel and recently arrived locals of southern Michigan no doubt had scarce knowledge of Michigan's original big cat—even as early as 1886.

Chapter 10

An Osceola Wild Cat

From the pages of the *Reed City Clarion*, of Reed City, Michigan, came a frightening account at the beginning of January, anno Domini 1900, of an extremely close encounter a woman and child had with a dangerous cat of the woods.

Over the previous two years, people—kids especially—in the vicinity of Deer Lake, Osceola County, Michigan, had become fearful of some "wild beast" prowling about the area. Its "screeching" was heard during the quiet of night, and several persons had "seen a long, gaunt form sneaking along the edge of the timber" at dusk.

Much livestock—fowl, young pigs, and lambs—vanished, only to have their bones subsequently discovered in the nearby timber. More than one hunting party was organized to search for and destroy the offending beast, but to no avail. Children were too scared to go to school.

"Strong men trembled when they heard that awful screech," claimed the *Clarion*, but "happily this is all changed now, for the animal has been killed," the paper added. The Sunday afternoon prior, a Mrs. Aginsold, residing on the "outskirts" of Deer Lake, went with her "little daughter" to the edge of the forest to locate and bring home a stray cow. The child was ahead of her mother and entered into a thicket. Just then a "blood-curdling shriek" split the air.

For an instant, Mom froze in her tracks. However, maternal instincts kicked in and the woman darted into the underbrush where she had seen her daughter disappear. What Mrs. Aginsold then witnessed shocked her to the core. The young girl was standing on a knoll, "transfixed with horror," as she watched just feet away, crouched on a low tree branch, a "hideous, horrible, animal."

The creature's tail "was lashing the limb in fury" and it was about to pounce upon the girl. At that moment mother screamed at her child to run. However, not waiting for her daughter to flee, the woman ran forward and found herself between her babe and the menacing brute. Mrs. Aginsold's protective move was just in the nick of time, for she instantly intercepted the "weight of the huge beast" as it landed on her back and shoulders.

Mother Aginsold considered herself a goner; however, the instant the fangs of the creature started fastening onto the back of her neck, a rifle shot rang out. The animal released its grip, let out a "mournful shriek" and fell dead at the woman's feet. The lady's eyes quickly glanced around, and to her total and grateful surprise, she spotted her husband standing a short distance away. The man had heard the loud commotion and wasted little time in arriving at the scene of the attack to save his wife and daughter.

The "much dreaded" and highly sought-after animal proved to be an enormous "wild cat," the news account stated. Reportedly the dead feline's body was taken to Grand Rapids, Michigan, to be handed over to a taxidermist.

Like so many of these fascinating old stories, this one too leaves the reader and researcher perplexed and with several questions. The most salient one, in this case, is whether the marauding cat was an actual panther or a wildcat, i.e., bobcat or lynx. The panther and wildcat, though different species of feline, were quite often referred to as the same animal way back in the day, e.g., sometimes real panthers/cougars were called "wildcats."

This printed story labels the animal in question as a "wild cat." However, it is highly unlikely a single bobcat or lynx (there is little difference between the two animals in size and appearance) would cause such fear and dread among a community of people and for so long. Historically, though both bobcat and lynx are known to have attacked humans, the occasions are extremely rare—far fewer than even the rare cougar attacks on people. A large bobcat or lynx is about one-fourth or one-fifth the weight of a large panther/cougar/mountain lion/puma.

Also, if the newspaper writer was correct, in that the animal's tail was "lashing" the tree limb which it was perched upon "in fury," it is not too possible the beast was a wildcat (bobcat or lynx) because these cats lack the tremendously long tail a panther possesses. They have short stubs for tails—not much capable of lashing anything.

Finally, the written account states the cat as being a "huge beast." Although there is the possibility the feline's size was exaggerated, if the description was right, little chance remains for bobcat or lynx, since they are rather small. A full-grown panther is a huge cat—and that is the only other realistic possibility regarding Michigan's naturally occurring kitties.

Though there is a dearth of information in the article regarding the particular feline's physical appearance, this author has come to the conclusion that the offending cat was indeed a panther and not either one of only two other possibilities—bobcat or lynx, commonly but not always accurately called "wildcat" way back when.

Chapter 11

William Sisco's Mortal Combat

Richard Hasbrook Sr. was for some time during the 1930s head of the United States government's historical Writer's Project for Gogebic County, Michigan. This program was part of the Works Progress Administration (WPA), one of numerous New Deal federal legislative initiatives established by President Franklin Delano Roosevelt and the United States Congress during the Great Depression. The goal, like all other "alphabet soup" programs of the 1930s, was to get unemployed American citizens working again through performance in much-needed enterprises. The writer's project was created in part to interview regular American citizens from all walks of life in order to record their personal experiences.

Mr. Hasbrook was likely a natural choice to lead the program in his neck of the woods, as he was one of the pioneer settlers of Gogebic County. His knowledge of the region and its people was vast. By 1941, however, the man had relocated to the state of California.

One of Hasbrook's interviews and subsequent written stories was of a personal friend, William Sisco, a local trapper who was attacked by a panther, circa 1906. Sisco at the time lived in Marenisco, Michigan, a tiny town in Gogebic County, the state's farthest western county of the Upper Peninsula.

Hasbrook revealed that one day, while trapping in the wild about six miles northeast of another small town—Bessemer, Michigan—also located in Gogebic County, Sisco was leaped upon by a huge cat which had been eyeing him from an overhanging tree. The beast landed on the unwary man's back and the two hit the ground. A tremendous battle ensued as both man and beast literally fought against one another for their very futures. Mr. Sisco did not have a firearm with him at the time, but did possess a trusty hunting knife which proved faithful. After a "fierce fight," the panther was killed.

The winner of the bloody affair, William Sisco, was not necessarily the clear victor, however, as the outdoorsman sustained horrific wounds from the cougar's teeth and claws. The terribly mauled trapper was in time able to make his way to Bessemer, where he was administered lifesaving treatment at the local hospital. Apparently though, Sisco never really fully recovered, as he was ever after plagued by rheumatism which was believed to have originated from the wounds inflicted by the huge cat's claws. The man suffered at length for years and eventually moved in with his sister, who resided in Holland, Michigan, located in the southwestern portion of Michigan's Lower Peninsula.

Recent efforts to learn more about William Sisco and the panther assault on him have proven fruitless. Tedious attempts to locate Richard Hasbrook Sr.'s original WPA account of the harrowing encounter have also been futile. The Library of Congress, National Archives, and the Smithsonian Institution, all of which house preserved WPA writings, were checked. Hasbrook definitely wrote for the WPA—that much is known—but the original account of the highly dramatic event mentioned above (from a secondary source) remains elusive, much like Michigan's remaining big cats of today.

Absent a credible debunking, the account of the ferocious panther attack on William Sisco, in the wilds of the western Upper Peninsula of Michigan, stands firm to this day.

PART V
A DOUBTFUL DISAPPEARANCE

Killed Big Catamount

Chapter 12

Nine Lives Expended

The January 3, 1907, front page headline of the *Sault Ste. Marie (Michigan) News* hollered out: "Killed Big Catamount," with the subheading stating, "Local Nimrods Have Exciting Time in Woods." The nimrods (hunters) were teenagers Chase Osborn Jr. and Ted LaLonde. Early Sunday, on December 30, 1906, the two set out from Deerfoot Lodge, a hunting clubhouse in western Chippewa County of Michigan's Upper Peninsula, near the scenic Tahquamenon River.

The youths were on a mission to inspect traps that had been placed at various spots in the vicinity. To their amazement, the boys discovered that one of the traps held a mammoth cat—a catamount, more commonly known in the modern era as cougar or mountain lion. After recovering from their initial shock, the teens snapped five photos of the unlucky creature and then shot it with a rifle.

However, only three bullets were fired, which was all that the young men had with them. The Sault Ste. Marie paper reported: "All three cartridges seemed to do little more than arouse the ire of the beast. The proverbial 'nine lives' story was certainly holding good. With all of the cartridges gone and the catamount showing even more life than at the beginning of the operation there remained nothing for the boys to do but to return five miles back to Deerfoot for a supply of ammunition. Upon their return to the scene with plenty of ammunition they experienced little difficulty in robbing the cat even of its nine lives, but their astonishment increased when they discovered that the brute had utterly destroyed a large No. 4 wolf-trap of the Newhouse make, literally breaking the jaws to pieces, leaving itself free so far as the trap was concerned."

This incident, though certainly newsworthy in its own right, was guaranteed print in the *Sault Ste. Marie News* because one of the two teens involved—Chase Osborn Jr.—was the son of the paper's former editor, Chase Osborn Sr. In fact, it was Chase Sr. who had actually set the trap which caught the big cat. The elder Osborn had ironically recently finished serving a term as the state game and fish warden, and would in just a few years, 1910, be elected governor of Michigan.

The pelt of the catamount was given as a gift to Michigan State Supreme Court Justice and former State Attorney General Charles Austin Blair. Blair was a son of Michigan's venerated "war" governor, Austin Blair, who served as the state's chief executive during the tumultuous years of the nation's long and bloody Civil War.

In a letter dated January 2, 1907, Michigan's future governor Chase Osborn Sr. wrote Justice Blair:

> My dear Judge Blair: - You may, perhaps, remember that I told you I would try to catch you a lynx. Well, I stayed in camp until Dec. 15, and put out traps there because [sons] George and Chase agreed to go out and look after them and get them during the holidays. They did so, and Mrs. Osborn

and I visited them last Monday. We were surprised and of course delighted to find hanging on the pole an immense cat animal. It is a kind of lynx, ... and both Lydekker and the International Encyclopedia describe it very accurately as a catamount. The boys shot the thing up quite a little, but the skin can be sewn up so that as a rug it will be whole and all right. ... Please keep it as a trophy of Deerfoot until you kill one yourself, and then you can pass it on to your first friend if you wish. Yours very sincerely, Chase S. Osborn

Judge Charles Austin Blair was apparently quite thrilled with the exotic and highly unusual gift via Mr. Osborn's magnificent gesture of friendship. The justice wrote back to him expressing utmost gratitude in a letter dated January 5, 1907:

Dear Mr. Osborn: -
The skin of the catamount arrived in good condition yesterday. ... I concluded to have it mounted in the form of a rug, since I rather inferred from your letter that it would make up better in that form. I have also received the clipping from the Soo News, giving an account of the capture, which made me very envious of the boys to be enabled to participate in such a combat. ... I am very much pleased with the gift and thank you and your sons very much for it. I can scarcely secure one by my own efforts, and I shall prize this the more highly. ... I do not know of anything you could have sent me which would have been more satisfactory to me, and my sole regret is that I am unable to reciprocate, unless you are willing to accept a great abundance of good will and friendship.

It was not immediate, but eventually this specific catamount or cougar, so tortuously slain near the Tahquamenon River in the end days of A.D. 1906, came to be regarded as the very last wild one of its kind in the state of Michigan. Nearly all state game officials, outdoor writers, and news personnel in general bought into the notion that this was the truth concerning the state's *Felis concolor*.

Why or how this came to be is a major curiosity because the belief or assumption is completely absurd and foolhardy—if not idiotic. How could any imaginative person conclude that panthers, i.e., cougars, mountain lions, pumas, catamounts, whatever one wishes to call them, were extirpated from Michigan via the killing of this particular specimen in the waning days of 1906?

The answer to the question should be obvious—there was and is no way of knowing. Some people probably knew better than to accept the narrative, especially members of John Q. Public, yet the claim became conventional wisdom. I especially know this because I've read the line (that the slain big cat of 1906 was the last of its kind in Michigan) dozens and dozens if not hundreds of times in the past quarter century. This take appeared in an untold number of periodicals, and absent the distinction, "last *known* cougar."

Without question Michigan's native big cat was considerably reduced in specimens over the decades, beginning with white settlement. This is undeniable. Many hundreds were hunted, trapped, and killed due to their common predations on livestock and the powerful creature's occasional attacks on humans. The massive clearing of so much acreage and subsequent settlement of thousands of people expanded human civilization, taking a tremendous toll on the animal.

However, the claim that all cougars were gone upon this particular ensnared Upper Peninsula big cat (at the end of 1906) being dispatched cannot be seriously accepted. This line of demarcation is totally arbitrary and therefore ridiculous.

Chase Salmon Osborn Sr. (January 22, 1860–April 11, 1949) had an illustrious career in Michigan as a businessman and prominent Republican politician. For many years he was the owner and editor of the *Sault News* (now the *Sault Ste. Marie [Michigan] Evening News*) and during that time was appointed to serve as Michigan's state fish and game warden. Osborn went on to become the state's commissioner of railroads and then became a member of the University of Michigan Board of Regents. In 1910 Chase S. Osborn Sr. was elected to a single term as Michigan governor, 1911–1913, becoming the state's first and only chief executive from the Upper Peninsula. It was he who in late December of 1906 actually set the wolf trap that snared Michigan's so-determined "last" cougar/catamount, which soon after was discovered and shot dead by 18-year-old son Chase S. Osborn Jr. and his teen friend Ted LaLonde. *Photos courtesy of the Bentley Historical Library, Ann Arbor, Michigan.*

Photo of Deerfoot Lodge in western Chippewa County, Michigan, not far from the famous Tahquamenon Falls, near where Michigan's "last" wild cougar was slain. *Photo courtesy of the Bentley Historical Library, Ann Arbor, MI.*

Charles Austin Blair (April 10, 1854–August 30, 1912) was a son of Michigan's highly esteemed "War Governor," Austin Blair (1818–1894), who skillfully and tirelessly mustered the state's citizens, farms, and factories for the Union cause during the U.S. Civil War (1861–1865). Charles followed his father into politics, eventually becoming Michigan's attorney general (1903–1905) and a justice on the state supreme court from 1905 until his death in 1912. While on the high court, Judge Blair received the catamount pelt of Michigan's "last" wild cougar from Chase S. Osborn Sr. as a token of friendship. The animal had just recently been killed by Osborn's son, Chase Jr. and his friend Ted LaLonde in the waning days of 1906. *Photo courtesy of the Bentley Historical Library, Ann Arbor, Michigan.*

Large pockets of wilderness have always existed within the state despite the clearing of massive tracts of land over time, either for farming or during the many years of major lumbering operations. Deer, the big cat's main staple, were always abundant enough, whether waxing or waning in population, to keep a certain amount of native cougars alive and reproducing in Michigan.

Short of ever having had an annual or semiannual canvassing of nearly every square mile of the state, with tens of thousands of citizen volunteers walking side by side at the same time (a logistical impossibility) to flush the beasts out, one can never seriously or truthfully claim the native panther/cougar/mountain lion/puma/catamount as ever being wiped clean from Michigan soil. To do so would, and should, invite incredible dismay, if not outright mockery.

Chapter 13

Upper Peninsula Evidence

State of Michigan trappers had earnestly been trying to capture a mountain lion (and were continuing in the endeavor), supposedly stalking the Huron Mountains of Michigan's Upper Peninsula, reported the *Detroit Free Press* and *Ironwood (Michigan) Daily Globe* in late 1933.

The Huron Mountains are located immediately south of Lake Superior in the extreme northwestern part of Marquette County, Michigan, about 40 miles away from the city of Marquette.

Evidence of a panther's presence in the region included "fleeting glances" from people, "large cat-like" tracks found along rivers, and carcasses of recently killed deer. Initially trappers thought the animal or animals in question to be a big Canadian lynx, but soon rejected the belief, saying the paw prints were way too big and that it was rare for a lynx to attack and kill "mature" deer, as with the current cases.

Albert Stoll Jr., of Ironwood's *Daily Globe*, on November 20, 1933, wrote: "In all probability it will be found that we have a puma or North American panther in our midst," before going on to mention the big cat as being native to the state. "However," he claimed, "there has been no evidence of the existence of pumas in Michigan of late years."

Therefore, Mr. Stoll speculated, one may have ventured into the state's Upper Peninsula via Wisconsin and Minnesota. If so, the Huron Mountains were an ideal place for such a creature to make its home, the man stated. Whether the newsman thought it was possible for an original, remnant population of cougars to still exist in this given U.P. region of Michigan as late as 1933, the fellow did not say—though locals within the area likely believed the native cougar status to be true.

Adding strength to the belief by state game personnel that at least a cougar or two dwelled in the Huron Mountains in the early 1930s (and beyond) was an investigation of all fauna in the region conducted by zoologist Richard H. Manville of Michigan State College (today's Michigan State University). Manville's research was sponsored by the Huron Mountain Club, a private organization then in possession of approximately 15,000 acres of real estate within the tremendously remote and wild tract of land.

Regarding his study, the professor noted that the mountain lion, or panther, was considered by those in the know to have been absent from Michigan since about 1900. However, the researcher recorded an abundance of (then) recent, credible evidence indicating the large cat's current presence in the Huron Mountain region. The findings seriously questioned the long-standing wisdom of the day that the panther of Michigan had been wiped out for some 30 to 40 years already.

Manville stated that at least three deer were known to have been killed and cached in characteristic cougar style near the private club in the fall of 1932. A man possessed a photograph of one of the cache kills, taken near Pine Lake. Additionally, in 1937 a very large cat with a long tail was seen by several persons over many weeks into the month of August. The zoologist wrote: "H. E. Perkins saw it, once at close range, on three occasions near the Yellow Dog Swamp; it was reported along the Salmon Trout River by Mrs. Raymond E. Durham, Richard Turner, and Walter Krieg; workmen at the M-35 Cabin reported it; it was seen by Onnie Peura at Pine Lake; Prof. G. E. Nichols heard what he was convinced was a cougar at Mountain Lake. Harry Boulden of Big Bay claimed to have shot it, but it disappeared into the Yellow Dog Swamp; at any event, it was not subsequently reported. This cat was thought to have killed and cached at least one deer, near the Skeet Field."

Professor Manville ended his listing of big cat witnesses by stating: "On July 14, 1940, Dr. Charles P. Drury and party reported seeing a cougar in the cutover land east of Conway Lake. On July 7, 1941, Howard Paul and party reported another near Big Bay."

In his conclusion Mr. Manville wrote that the last two reports mentioned by him "may well have been cases of mistaken identity." Why he stated this, but did not do so regarding the prior sightings, is not known. However, the investigator's skepticism speaks positively of the overall study. All good researchers need to have a certain amount of doubt regarding whatever data they come up with. To strengthen one's case, on whatever the subject, investigators must be ready to dismiss or debunk any evidence which appears questionable. Like with any sizeable recording of alleged events, there will always exist a credibility continuum. Evidence gathered is obviously not going to be of equal value in all situations or cases.

William H. Burt was a noted zoologist at the University of Michigan. When writing about the mammals of the Great Lakes region in his book from 1957, *Mammals of the Great Lakes Region*, Burt declared the mountain lion/cougar/panther "gone from the local fauna" but offered the caveat: "Although there is still a remote chance that it may persist in small numbers in the northern part of the area."

Where exactly Professor Burt meant by the "northern part" of the region is a matter of speculation because he gives no specific place or places—the natural assumption is Michigan's Upper Peninsula, or perhaps even the northern Lower Peninsula. But Burt may have meant outside of the state of Michigan completely, e.g., north of Lake Superior and Lake Huron in the Canadian province of Ontario.

If he meant the Upper Peninsula of Michigan and maybe the northern Lower Peninsula too, Burt was likely both correct and incorrect—correct to leave open the possibility the big cat still roamed in parts of Michigan, because they almost certainly did, but incorrect to say small numbers—unless he considered "small numbers" to be at least a few dozen instead of literally a few animals of one, two, three, or four.

During the same year William Burt published his book on mammals of the Great Lakes (1957) claiming there to be a "remote chance" of cougars still existing in the North Country, a flurry of big cat sightings occurred in Michigan's eastern Upper Peninsula. The viewings had actually been taking place in the region since at least 1954.

A United Press article from early April 1958 picked up by the *Holland Evening Sentinel,* of Holland, Michigan, reported that a "Phantom Panther" of Michigan's Chippewa County had been seen "numerous times" in the fall of 1957 but seemed to have disappeared during the winter months of 1957 and 1958. However, that was until Rudyard, Michigan, resident Uno Hendrickson stepped forward with a claim which had him encountering the "six-foot beast" while trapping about 20 miles southwest of Sault Ste. Marie, Michigan, in early April of 1958.

According to Hendrickson, the cat "bounded out an open door

of an empty barn" only 20 feet from him and ran off into the forest. The large feline's tail was about three feet in length. The woodsman stated: "It turned its vicious big yellow eyes at me." The trapper then admitted to being "frightened," as he was unarmed.

The previous fall, 1957, Hendrickson got off a failed long-distance shot at the panther after spotting it in the wild. A "panther posse" was organized and went in search of the animal, but was unable to locate a single track.

Fast forward 14 years from 1958. The "Mystery Cat," i.e., cougar, panther, catamount, of the eastern Upper Peninsula, was said to be making its presence known again among local citizens, wrote the *Evening News* of Sault Ste. Marie in an article dated November 27, 1972.

On November 20, 1972, Walter Waggner, from the Saginaw region, allegedly heard the death throes of a dying buck while near the edge of the huge Gogomain Swamp, in the eastern U. P., by Munuscong Bay. Some hours later, Waggner was able to locate the "few grisly" remains of the deer. It had been eaten almost entirely by a "beast or beasts unknown," though it was cat tracks that were said to be found at the killing site, according to the newspaper.

The news story went on to say that the "Mystery Cat" was first witnessed and reported 18 years earlier by a "minister" on September 17, 1954, at a place dubbed "Mission Hill," west of Sault Ste. Marie. Following that noteworthy incident, more than 100 other persons came forward to the *Evening News* and reported similar sightings of the big cat or cats. The beast was supposedly spotted at numerous localities in Chippewa, Luce, and Mackinac counties, "at both regular and sporadic intervals" throughout the current and previous years. The lion's share of the sightings (no pun intended) occurred within a 20-mile radius of a place named Rock View Hills, south of Pickford, Michigan, off Highway M-129, claimed the newspaper.

If the November 1972 deer-killing incident was indeed the work of a cougar, it would be close to impossible for it to be the same animal or of the same big cats allegedly prowling the eastern U.P. from 1954 to late 1958. Fifteen or 16 years is the maximum life span for a mountain lion living in the great outdoors. Could the supposed '72 big cat be offspring of the alleged '54–'58 panther or panthers? It is entirely plausible. If so, it obviously indicates a breeding population of cougars in the eastern Upper Peninsula over many years. It is also possible the alleged eastern U.P. cougars from the 1950s and early 1970s, respectively, were unrelated or not immediately related. Either scenario lends credence to the powerful hypothesis that Michigan's native panthers were never completely extirpated from their home soil.

This theory is bolstered by continued eyewitness reports and other evidence of cougars present in the eastern Upper Peninsula from the late 1970s and beyond. In the early fall of 1978, an outdoorsman near Strongs, Michigan, a village about 25 miles west of Sault Ste. Marie in the eastern Upper Peninsula, claimed to have come within close view of a cougar while on foot. Supposedly the cat left serious but nonlethal wounds on the man's beagle. The dog ventured out of the owner's yard the day before, but had not returned home soon after as on all other previous occasions when loose. While walking a desolate two-track road in search of his pet, the man, who refused to give his name out of fear of ridicule, spotted a huge creature. It was the size of a large dog, but with a longer body, he told outdoor writer George Rintamaki. The fellow's description continued: "It was tawny yellow in color and had the round short-eared head of a cat. Its shoulders were massive and the legs appeared to be somewhat heavier than those of a dog. Its tail was long, arched up near the body, then dropped to the ground."

Rintamaki wrote in response to the man's statement: "This is a letter-perfect description of a cougar or mountain lion," and further noted that the anonymous man was a woodsman "of many years experience" who knew the difference between what he'd seen and all other animals of the region.

The beagle, which eventually came home on its own, was in rough shape. Bloodied, it was discovered to have had one of its eyes nearly gouged out and an ear torn off. The claw marks left on the hound definitely appeared to be from a large cat.

The man who had the impressive sighting and who nearly lost his dog made plaster casts of the animal's tracks. Wrote Rintamaki: "They appear to be those of a large member of the cat family," before mentioning how cats rarely leave nail marks in their tracks because their claws are retractable, whereas a canine will usually show nail marks in their prints because their claws cannot retract.

Before concluding his article on the eastern U.P.'s "mystery cat," the author mentions that a Newberry (Michigan) restaurant owner claimed to have shot a couple of rounds from a high-powered deer rifle at a "cougar-like" beast 20 years earlier (circa 1958) in wilderness known as the "Sage Swamp" but missed his target. With its long tail, the animal "looked to be eight feet long."

Further evidence of the panther never having disappeared from Michigan comes from two state employees in 1966. Conservation officers Francis Opolka and Al Konkel of the Michigan Department of Natural Resources were driving a vehicle in Delta County, not far from the town of Cornell in the south-central Upper Peninsula. It was approximately 2:30 a.m. and raining when the men saw what looked like a cougar make its way across a paved road.

Turning a spotlight on the animal, the officers viewed it slowly cross a field close to them. At times the creature was within 50 feet of the truck. The next day, a state biologist made a plaster cast of one of the animal's tracks which showed it to be much larger than that of a bobcat. The cast was later examined by staff at the University of Michigan Museum; they declared it to be the print from a "large cat."

A year later in 1967, Opolka, who would eventually become

deputy director of the Michigan DNR, recorded in a report dated June 30, that there were at least two other cougar sightings from 1965–1967 in the same area. One took place only 15 miles northeast of Opolka and Konkel's big cat sighting, in southern Marquette County. Years later, Mr. Opolka declared: "There is really nothing else it could have been than a cougar."

Regarding Michigan's far western Upper Peninsula, Dave LaPointe worked for the Michigan state parks system in the 1960s and 1970s. He wrote that in 1967 a "rash of [big] cat sightings" were reported by members of the public in the Bessemer-Wakefield region close to the Michigan-Wisconsin border. The same year a Porcupine Mountains State Park interpreter said he witnessed a cougar cross Highway M-107 in the center of the nearly 60,000-acre preserve.

In 1970 Mr. LaPointe was assistant park manager at the Porcupine Mountains Park and was initially a "scoffer" at the suggestion of cougars still roaming Michigan's Upper Peninsula. However, after there had been a handful of supposed mountain lion sightings in the park that summer, with the most credible coming from two men saying they saw a cougar cross M-107 only a hundred feet in front of their truck "in broad daylight," doubter LaPointe opened himself up to the possibility of mountain lions in the region.

It was not long, though, before the state park ranger shifted from being open to the possibility to becoming a "true believer." One day during time off, LaPointe went hunting for grouse within the park off a main trail. The day was cold and wet. The fellow hiked from his pickup truck two-and-a-half miles to a picturesque body of water known as Mirror Lake. Damp clay on the pathway pulled at his boots.

Returning a couple hours later, LaPointe trekked back via the same route he had ventured in on. Something was different, however. The man's eyes could not avoid spotting large, fresh animal tracks in the moistened earth. The prints appeared to definitely be from a feline, and were positively not there during the hunter's earlier jaunt in. Measuring the tracks, LaPointe discovered they were three-and-a-half inches wide—much too large to be made by a bobcat. One of the big cat tracks was even embedded within one of LaPointe's boot prints.

The animal clearly had made its way on the same trail after the bird hunter passed through. Was it trailing him specifically? The man became unnerved at the thought, even though he told himself that cougars were shy animals and rarely dangerous to people.

Years later LaPointe wrote, "Whatever the validity of all those previous reports, I knew that there was at least one mountain lion that day walking Michigan's Porcupine Mountains."

After his unseen but close encounter with the big cat, Mr. LaPointe began to collect other reliable cougar sightings in Michigan's Upper Peninsula, compelling him to write: "The frequency of these sightings over the entire Upper Peninsula for at least fifteen years, leads me to believe that Michigan is home to more than just a single 'freak' stray."

For example, recorded LaPointe, in May of 1976 two DNR fisheries biologists saw a cougar scamper across U.S. 45 in front of their vehicle near "Military Hill" in Ontonagon County. The next day a logger from Alston, Michigan, claimed he saw a cougar run across Highway M-38 at the Firesteel River. Both sightings were only seven miles apart, leading to speculation it was the same animal. Not long after, in July of 1976, a forester for the Upper Peninsula Power Company, along with his wife, reported seeing a mountain lion near Paulding, Michigan.

The one-time skeptic, after much investigation and review, became without a doubt convinced the mountain lion still existed in Michigan's Upper Peninsula. But, inquired LaPointe, how so? The ranger offered up several possible explanations. One, the big cats may have come in from western states. Or, the cougar of Michigan never completely disappeared many decades prior, as was said to be

Frederick Nault snapped this picture of a mountain lion on May 12, 2012, at approximately 8 p.m. The massive-sized cat had crossed the highway in front of his vehicle on Ravine River Road near the Village of Skanee, Baraga County, Michigan. *Photo courtesy of Fred Nault.*

the case by virtually all wildlife experts. Maybe an original population did remain.

The investigator even left open the possibility of cougars roaming the state due to the escape or release of exotic pets from privately owned roadside zoos, or from individuals who owned the animals but found them too difficult to raise, therefore subsequently letting them loose into the wild. However, LaPointe admitted that he was doubtful of the "escaped" or "released" exotic pet explanation.

Quite like the experience of Dave LaPointe's conversion, Upper Peninsula of Michigan outdoors writer Don Maki became a believer in the cougar's existence within the state after initial doubt and skepticism. Maki's encounter with the mountain lion, also like

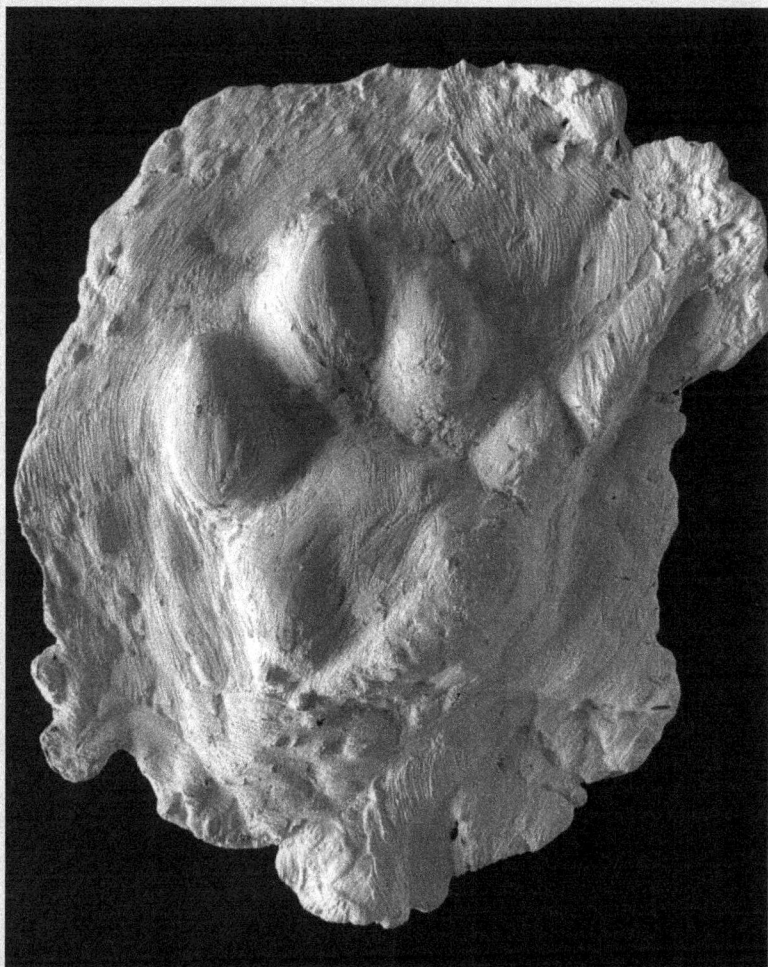

Nault returned soon after to make a plaster cast of one of the lion's large paw prints. This sighting occurred within the Upper Peninsula of Michigan's Huron Mountains, a region long suspected of harboring a hold-out population of native Michigan panthers. *Photo courtesy of Fred Nault.*

LaPointe's, occurred in the western U.P., but 20 years later, which is telling because it shows that large cat sightings by citizens never abated—again strengthening the theory of a remnant population.

Yet again like LaPointe, who was a State of Michigan conservation employee becoming a believer, and who cited other state officials as witnesses to the big feline, Maki too recounted several state wilderness officials as ending up mostly convinced the cougar dwelled in Michigan. He started with Dave Bowerman, a Michigan DNR conservation officer stationed in the U.P.'s Iron County. The man was a denier of the cougar's continuous natural presence in Michigan's Upper Peninsula, believing any free-roaming mountain lion as being a released or escaped pet. Stated Bowerman: "They are a long way from their range in the west," thus indicating the animal would have to travel an insurmountable distance and over terrain not typical of its habitat to get to the U.P. This was a key reason to dismiss the cat's presence.

However, the state official's strong skepticism was tempered by the words: "There was a [big cat] print found in the Marquette area some time back."

This was followed by another DNR official of Michigan, wildlife biologist Jim Hammill, stationed in the U.P., who claimed reports came in at least once a month of cougars being around. The officer stated that Wisconsin conservation official Ron Schultz, of that state's wolf recovery program, had trailed big cat tracks the previous winter (1993) for three miles along the Wisconsin and Michigan border. Schultz was said to have stated that the tracks could only have come from a cougar.

Writer Maki then brought up Michigan DNR forester Mike Zuidema's accounts of the big cat. The man, like virtually all others, had been a skeptic of panthers dwelling within Michigan. That was until he witnessed one in March of 1981 directly in front of him on Highway M-35 between Escanaba and Menominee, Michigan.

Zuidema, through the years, after much careful and highly detailed research, went on to present hundreds of pieces of evidence positively showing the mountain lion's existence in the Michigan U.P. His untold number of testimonials was capped by an incident from two hunters claiming they saw a cougar after arriving at a hunting camp gate in their truck (the fall of 1992). This was in the Stonington region. The cat crossed the road in front of them accompanied by five kittens.

Mr. Zuidema went on by saying a forestry employee less than a mile away also witnessed the mother cat and its "litter." Maki concluded his article by writing that several other cougar sightings took place in Iron County, Michigan, over the previous years, including another one of a big momma cat with several kittens. This happened near Amasa, Michigan.

Regarding his own sighting, Maki wrote that he had initially felt the same as many DNR persons who had "discounted" U.P. cougar claims from citizens. That was until October 31, 1990, when a friend from Caspian phoned and told him, "There's a cougar in my backyard."

The writer quickly grabbed a camera and, along with an acquaintance who had stopped by his workplace to chat, jumped into a vehicle and sped two miles to his friend's place of residence. Upon arriving, the woman told them that she had seen a cougar on the edge of her lawn no more than 100 feet from her house. Seeing nothing for quite a while, Maki became frustrated by his friend's claim. He began to feel doubtful even though he knew the woman and her husband to be honest and upright people—persons who would never lie. However, soon after looking from the woman's rear deck again, Maki's disenchantment instantly vanished when a large cat emerged into full view. Wrote Maki: "Suddenly, the big tawny cat with the round face, lithe body and long tail came into the opening."

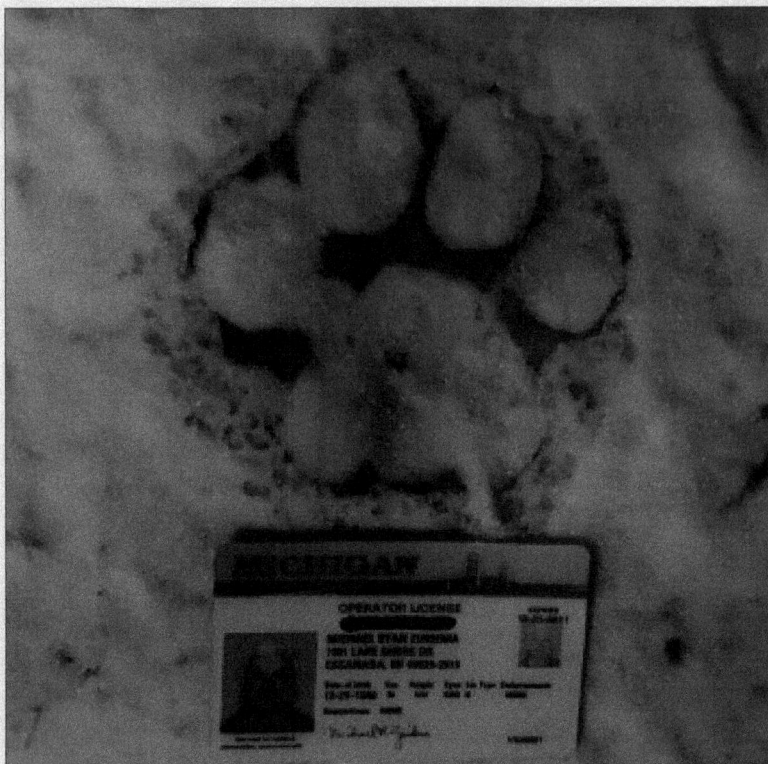

This mountain lion track was discovered along with others on March 11, 2008, by longtime Upper Peninsula of Michigan cougar researcher Mike Zuidema. The fresh prints were located in Delta County near Bark River, Michigan, approximately 15 miles southwest of Escanaba. The driver's license card was placed near the cat track to reference its size. This one measured about three-and-a-half inches wide and nearly four inches long—within standard diameter for an adult cougar of either sex. *Photo courtesy of Kile Zuidema.*

The critter was about 200 yards away and walking in a nonchalant manner. Maki felt he had a chance to retrieve his binoculars from his car. But when he returned, there was no time to line up his field glasses with his camera on the deck railing—"The rare visitor had entered some bushes, never to return."

🐾

Returning to the aforementioned Michigan wilderness official Dave LaPointe, the fellow believed that whatever the reason the native cat still stalked the Great Lakes State, its presence should be welcomed—even cherished. Describing heartfelt thoughts of the beast, through romantic sentiment most persons can relate to, he penned: "Place a mountain lion or a couple of wolves in a large wild tract and it becomes wilderness. You may never see them, but you know they're there, and knowing this, your own attitude toward the area changes. Take them away, however, and the place becomes something less. If Michigan really does have some mountain lions, aren't we better off for it?"

Chapter 14

Lower Peninsula Evidence

The *Cadillac News* of Cadillac, Michigan, stated in mid-November of 1916 that despite the town of Cadillac being an area of Michigan "well-settled," it was yet possible for an experienced hunter to kill many kinds of wild game in the region, including a panther. The newspaper claimed the word was out that a person need not "travel very far from Cadillac to find panther tracks." A large panther at the time resided in Cherry Grove Township, according to farmers there, and the big cat was said to have recently broken free from a trap, reported the paper.

Much further south, in mid-September 1921, Belding, Michigan, farmer Fayette Hoppough claimed that one of his cows had been attacked by a wild animal and that what he and several others witnessed appeared to be a panther. His report "caused quite a stir" among the citizens of the Belding community, wrote the *Belding Banner*. Hoppough and fellow believers surmised the animal "had roamed down into [their] section of the country from its northern home," but some locals thought the idea of a panther in the vicinity was "a lot of hot air being shot off."

Farmer Hoppough said that he fired a round at the animal and that it emitted a "weird human cry of pain or anger," then retreated "into the distance." The man stated that he believed the bullet struck one of the creature's feet.

The author of the *Banner* news article wrote that while there was little possibility the predatory animal was a real panther, older residents in the community gave testimonials that the big cat used to be in the area "in the early days"; therefore, in remote and wild parts of the state some of the creatures "might still be hiding," which made it possible for one to be able to "evade detection" until making its way "this far south."

Continued the newsman, "Mr. Hoppough sticks to the idea that there is no hot air about" the attacker of his cow likely being a panther and that because of his stance, the farmer was "getting considerable roasting" from his friends. Hoppough's response to his detractors was that although he wished them "no serious harm," he would like to see the alleged panther, "which tore his cow's tail off," make its presence known to them "and let 'em know that all panthers aren't dead yet, not by a long shot and that there is a possibility that one can get down here."

In addition to farmer Fayette Hoppough's experience, the *Banner* reported that area farmer Pete Upson recently had many of his sheep slain. The man was unable to pinpoint what exact animal the culprit was, or how many of his sheep were destroyed, as they were "scattered all over the woods of his farm." Though dogs were soon presumed to be responsible for the slaughter, Upson said he felt it was possible the source of the massacred sheep may have been from "the depredations of this panther."

The sheep were said to have all been killed in the same way, reported the paper, with a large hole torn in their sides in front of their hind legs and having the appearance of being gutted in the same act. Although the sheep killings in this situation looked to be the work of canines, which are known to sometimes disembowel their victims alive, cougars create cavities in the sides of their large prey too—as they instinctively zero in on vital organs for the tremendous nutrients they contain.

Whether or not the beast or beasts engaged in the Belding livestock attacks were a panther or dogs, it is interesting to note that the writer of the news article and his subjects imply, more than once, that panthers remained in northern Michigan as late as 1921—as if it was common knowledge. The only question of theirs appears to be whether or not the big cat would realistically visit as far south as Belding.

It seems, though, that there was at least one panther dwelling in the vicinity not far from Belding 36 years earlier, as reported by N. A. Wood and L. R. Dice in a joint scientific paper, "Records of the Distribution of Michigan Mammals," published in 1924.

An L. C. Hodges claimed that his dogs treed a panther just a little northeast of Belding near Stanton, in Montcalm County, Michigan, in 1885. The man was not able to kill the beast because he did not have a gun with him during the encounter.

If the creature that attacked Fayette Hoppough's cow was truly a panther, was it lineage of the Stanton panther treed in 1885? Questions arise: Does the big cat still roam the Belding area or only the Upper Peninsula and northern Lower Peninsula, if at all?

The late Nelson Yoder, longtime historian of Michigan's Montmorency, Oscoda, and Ogemaw counties, conducted a series of interviews in 1981 and 1982, in which he questioned many of the region's citizens to probe the possibility of the native cougar's continued presence. It all began when Yoder interviewed longtime local deer hunter Tony Schild of Kneeland, Michigan, in Oscoda County.

Schild had a lot of fabulous stories of his hunting prowess but what really piqued Yoder's curiosity was the hunter's mentioning of his big cat experiences.

Mr. Schild reminisced about an interesting happening from 40 Novembers earlier:

> It was in 1941, near West Branch [Ogemaw County], a [moon-lit] night and about three inches of snow on the ground—back then, hunters camped in tents, not motor homes and campers. … I was in the tent that night, and heard the most terrifying screams outside, as if someone were murdering a baby. I got the gun loaded and waited in the tent not know-ing exactly what to expect. The screams subsided and the next morning, I tracked what I say was a big cat for three miles down the middle of the fire lane. To this day, I believe that it was a mountain lion, or a cougar or a puma.

Tony Schild went on to say that his belief in having a genuine pan-ther encounter back in 1941 had been recently "verified" via a new big cat experience. The fellow told his interviewer Yoder that he had seen one in April of 1981. The cat strolled by his house on Perry Creek Road. Schild described it as about four feet long with a tail about three feet in length, "coming down to the ground in an 'S' curve."

Said Schild: "Its muscles were a rippling display of strength, and its color was honey blond."

As far as trying to get corroborating evidence for what he was seeing, Schild claimed that he was so "dumbstruck at the sight" it didn't occur to him to grab a gun or a camera. However, the man's wife, Betty, witnessed the entire large cat appearance along with him.

Deer hunter Tony Schild's big cat testimonials enthralled Nelson Yoder. His appetite now whetted for more nearby personal experiences with the Michigan cougar, the historian began investigating throughout the region.

Soon the local historian Yoder brought forth the experience of Mrs. Fern Perry of Mio, Michigan, who in late 1981 recounted a fascinating event from over 42 years earlier during the winter of 1939. The season was a harsh one. The young woman was staying at the family farm, later the Chuck Meering property, one mile south of Comins, Michigan. In the middle of the night, screaming from the outdoors pierced the terribly cold air. The shocking noise came from around the root cellar opening.

The moon was fairly bright, and in its illumination, Fern spotted from her window a very large cat at the cellar entrance. The creature looked like it was trying to enter the house to gain relief from the frozen conditions. Astonished, the young woman originally assumed the cat to be of the lynx sort, but then saw a long, curved tail attached to it. She quickly concluded that "it was obviously not a lynx or a bobcat."

Mrs. Perry's large cat sighting turned out to be just the first of two during her years living in the region. During the deer hunting season of 1943 or '44, Fern witnessed another cat "similar" to the one she saw in the winter of 1939. It happened in Mio around Ninth and Randall streets. A long tail extended from the honey-colored creature as it prowled within the town limits.

While continuing his investigation, Mr. Yoder interviewed an elderly widow, Ruth Taylor, who told him that a big cat was shot dead many years earlier near Greenwood Road, Ogemaw County, Michigan, in 1919. A hunting party of railroad men from Bay City, Michigan, encountered the cat while deer hunting and killed it in Horton Township. The animal weighed 165 pounds. One of the hunters posed with the creature's front paws and arms pulled over his shoulders while the lower part of the cat rested on the ground, said Taylor. Mr. Yoder did not indicate in his article whether Mrs. Taylor had actually witnessed the men with the slain cat personally or had only seen a picture of the dead beast.

Mrs. Taylor spoke on, saying that many years later, after moving not too far away to Mio, Michigan, she was witness to the cougar on more than one occasion. In June of 1966, around 6:30 p.m., the woman sighted a big cat at a small stream flowing through a culvert not far from her house. The animal was about the color of a deer and much larger than a dog. The cat slunk through the sizeable pipe and walked through a mud slick on the other side of the road, leaving visible tracks before passing over dry ground.

Yet another interesting incident was recalled by Taylor and reported to Yoder. The woman stated that one of her neighbors, a man with the last name of Handrich, discovered some (large) cat tracks in the snow during a winter in the early 1950s. The fellow carefully removed one of the snow imprints and transferred it to "Blumer's store" in Kneeland, where it was kept in a freezer for locals to come view. At about the same time (1953), Taylor found big cat tracks in the woods near her family's farm.

The lady was far from being finished with her fascinating accounts of the native big cat, stating she again witnessed the animal in 1977, and that her grand-daughter's husband did so as well in the winter of 1979 while snowshoeing in the area.

Reflecting on all these personal encounters, Mrs. Taylor opined: "I think the big cats have always been here, but they manage to stay out of sight most of the time."

Ruth Taylor's mentioning to historian Nelson Yoder her remembrance of a huge cat track being preserved by the efforts of a man slicing through the snow around it and taking it to a store's freezer was corroborated by a son of the man who did it. The fellow who protected the big feline snow print, so that others could bear witness to it, was Jacob Handrich. The man's son, Dwight Handrich, was questioned by Yoder and had this to say: "In 1954, or about the time there were actual sightings, Dad found the tracks in the snow and thought to dig one up and preserve it in Blumer's freezer. I went with him on one of these cat tracking excursions and the path seemed to parallel the Au Sable River east to west following the ridge above Comins Flats. The trail led in the direction of the Blockhouse Swamp."

Mr. Yoder later interviewed several other local citizens from the counties where he spent his youth and most adult years, accumulating even more significant evidence indicating the ongoing existence of the cougar in Michigan's Lower Peninsula through all decades of the 20th century.

An especially interesting testimonial came from a man named Mike Sarnes, who told Yoder that in October 1982 he and a hunting partner strolled up on three big cats "perched" on top of a wind-fallen tree. Sarnes was so surprised at the sight he could hardly believe his eyes because the animals were definitely not large feral or stray house cats. The two hunters watched the trio of felines in total dismay for about five minutes before all three wandered off. Mr. Sarnes described the cats as big as a good-sized Labrador retriever dog. Said Sarnes: "It is my opinion that the trio consisted of a female and two young cubs, three-fourths grown ... during my observation, they did not make a sound; the two smaller cats left the tree first—these I think were the cubs. The largest cat was approximately four feet long."

After his wondrous experience, Mike Sarnes said that he returned to the place of the cougar sightings six times, hoping to spot the cats again, or find a den, but never had any luck. What is incredibly significant though, is that the man's sighting of a mother cougar with two cubs spelled out big cats of a native population, rather than mountain lions released by humans or just wandering through.

Regarding Nelson Yoder, the man undeniably performed an invaluable service to the public, and especially nature lovers, by way

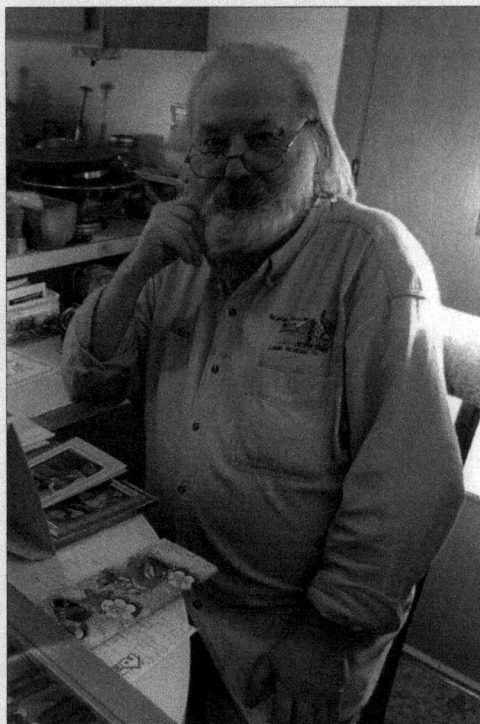

Nelson Yoder, Dec. 7, 1940–June 10, 2018.
Photo courtesy of Romona Blouin, sister of Nelson.

of his numerous documentations (via modern-day testimonials) of the Michigan panther's continued existence in a sizeable portion of the Lower Peninsula all through the decades of the 20th century. The sheer volume of what he gathered on the subject completely flies in the face of the official line from numerous "experts" who, without ever questioning, dutifully lined up over the years to claim the big cat long gone from the Great Lakes State's Lower Peninsula.

To even call Yoder's collection of evidence "invaluable" amounts to a major understatement regarding the tremendous service performed by him on behalf of our growing knowledge of one of the State of Michigan's native apex predators. For the work in which he diligently partook, we are forever grateful. Rest in peace, Nelson.

PART VI
MODERN-DAY PROOF THE PANTHER
STILL PROWLS MICHIGAN

A cougar track discovered in Michigan in the early 2000s. *Photo courtesy of Dr. Patrick Rusz.*

Chapter 15

The Rusz Investigation

The Michigan Wildlife Conservancy (originally the Michigan Wildlife Habitat Foundation) is a private, nonprofit organization that was established in 1982 with the mission of protecting and restoring wetlands and other natural areas inside the state. Documenting the continued existence of rare or endangered animals within the Michigan landscape is another one of the group's activities.

For well over three years beginning in 1999, in both upper and lower peninsulas of Michigan, 297 scats resembling cougar droppings were collected in 12 areas by Dr. Patrick J. Rusz of the Michigan Wildlife Conservancy. Various eager volunteers often accompanied Dr. Rusz. The team of wildlife sleuths investigated places that had a history of alleged big cat sightings.

Dr. Rusz and fellow colleagues of the MWC, as well as interested members of the public, had all shared the same "hunch" that Michigan's native cougar, considered long gone by experts, still roamed the forests, swampland, and riverine areas of much of the state. So a major investigation was launched by the conservation outfit with Rusz at its lead.

After considerable research, much of it field work, Rusz, et al., concluded that a relatively small, remnant population of cougars existed within both of the state's big peninsulas. The findings were announced in a professional publication issued by the MWC.

Mr. Rusz and his preservation organization, however, soon came under fire from state game officials within the Department of Natural Resources and others for daring to pronounce that a native stock of mountain lions still roamed Upper and Lower Michigan. The disagreement was mostly professional or academic in nature but at times turned personal—derisive in fact. The official line from the DNR in the early 2000s was that it was extremely doubtful wild cougars still existed within the state. Any mountain lion in the out-of-doors, the agency said, was more than likely an escaped or released exotic pet that had been held in captivity.

Critics of Dr. Rusz were quick to point out that the professional paper he presented, after the research was complete, had not been peer-reviewed and published in a scientific wildlife journal. So the wildlife biologist, ever-the-more determined and highly convinced by his and the group's volunteer discoveries, speedily went to work.

DNA testing was done on the scat samples. Some testing had already occurred, but more was completed. Dr. Rusz enlisted Bradley J. Swanson of Central Michigan University for the DNA analysis. To serve as units of comparison against Rusz's collected scats, Swanson also tested the DNA from tissue samples of known bobcats, cougars, coyotes, and wolves. Another DNA sample to compare with came from a partial tooth sawed off from a cougar skull unearthed in 1966. The big cat cranium had been buried with the remains of four Native American children. The burial site of the young ones was discovered by accident in Michigan's Saginaw County on farmland atop a ridge along the Flint River (see the Prelude).

Some of the tests were shown to be conclusive and were then subsequently peer-reviewed in the affirmative for publication in the scientific journal *The American Midland Naturalist*. The many years of study, research, and investigation engaged in by Rusz proved fruitful. The man was vindicated. However, the breakthrough investigator never received a "mea culpa" from his critics. It behooved them to admit he was correct. But, oh well, I digress ...

So, what were the results? Of the nearly 300 scats gathered, 12 were genetically determined to be from specific known animals. Of the 12, 10 were shown to be from cougars, one from another cat—the bobcat—and the other one from a canine—species unknown. The remaining 285 scats were unable to be genetically recognized and therefore could not be matched to the fauna which produced them. However, it is highly likely many of those unreadable waste specimens actually did come from cougars; unfortunately, we will never know with certainty. One can only speculate.

Because twice it was determined the same cat (but different from each other) could have produced two of the 10 scats due to certain droppings being found in close proximity, Rusz and Swanson cautiously concluded that, "there were at least 8 [different] cougars in Michigan, over the three years of this study."

Four of the eight cougars were Upper Peninsula cats—one each from the counties of Houghton, Dickinson, Menominee, and Delta. Four of the eight cougars were Lower Peninsula cats—one each from the counties of Emmet, Presque Isle, Alcona, and Roscommon.

These determinations were incredibly significant, though one may be forgiven for wondering out loud: Why did so many scats produce no readable DNA and thus no source of the animal they came from?

Whether it be the handling of the most delicate and fragile of Michigan's native wildlife or examining evidence of the continued existence of one of the Wolverine State's most ferocious apex predators, Dr. Patrick Rusz has experienced the full continuum of Michigan's natural environment. Sadly, the researcher has been treated with both derision and contempt for daring to postulate via his findings that Michigan still retains an original, native stock of big cats—the panther, cougar, mountain lion, puma, etc.—whatever one wishes to call them. *Photo courtesy of Dr. Patrick Rusz.*

Dr. Rusz fully admitted:

"The age of our scat samples is the most likely explanation for our inability ... we did not use a systematic searching of a given area to obtain the freshest scats. Our sampling method was a haphazard sampling of areas and we collected all scat samples regardless of age. This collection technique resulted in our collecting many scats that had been exposed to the environment for unknown, but often, long periods of time. Thus, the majority of our scat samples had likely been exposed to several freeze-thaw cycles and extensive amounts of precipitation and UV radiation, all of which degrade DNA."

Another interesting and telling part of Rusz and Swanson's overall study conclusion was summed up by their statement that, "Our

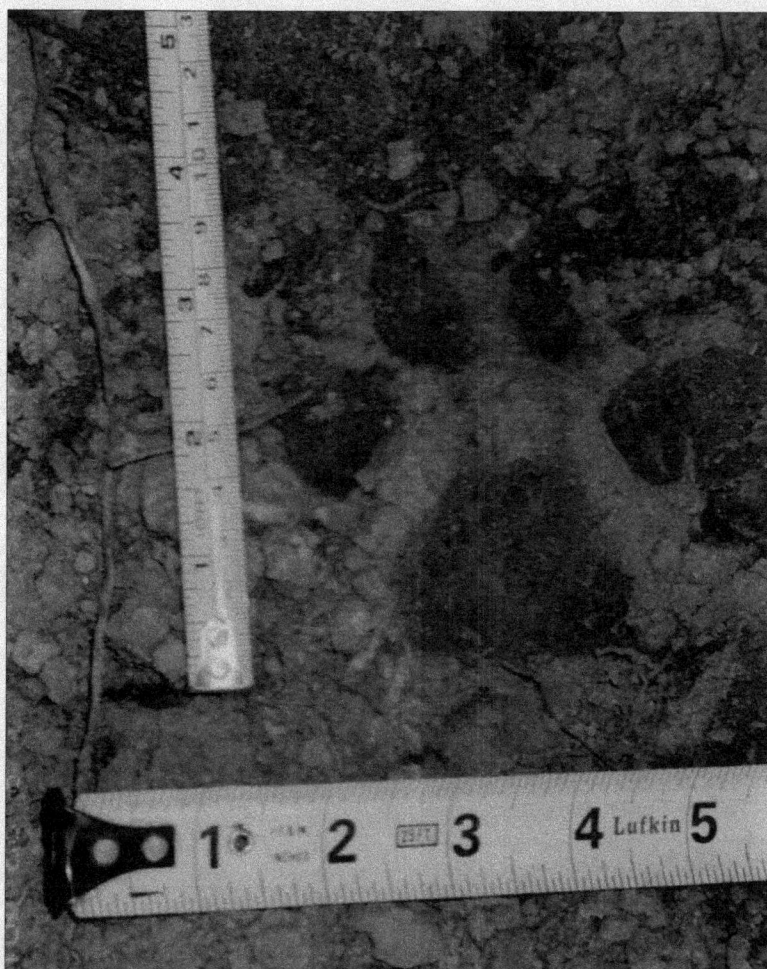

Dale Willy raised horses. He lives near Tower, Michigan, in Cheboygan County very close to the Cheboygan County and Presque Isle County, Michigan, border line. On a summer day in 2001, Willy thought he saw an extremely large cat on his property. However, what he glimpsed had disappeared so quickly that Willy could not be certain as to what creature had actually been there. Then, a couple of days after the mysterious sighting, a newborn foal completely vanished from a corral. Mr. Willy welcomed an investigation by the then-Michigan Wildlife Habitat Foundation who sent forth wildlife biologist Dr. Patrick Rusz. Tracks were soon discovered and photographed, revealing textbook cougar prints. The above photo is one that was taken. *Photo courtesy of Dr. Patrick Rusz.*

data show that there are no genetic differences in the sequence of a historical cougar sample from Michigan '*or* from a contemporary Michigan cougar' compared to cougars currently resident elsewhere in North America."

Why is this "telling?" Because of the "escaped pet" theory. As mentioned earlier, personnel from the Michigan DNR and other naysayers had persistently claimed for years that if Michigan had some cougars roaming about, they were likely escaped or released exotic pets and therefore not native animals. Tie this to the fact it is known that the exotic pet trade was historically, if not exclusively, stocked with cougars from South America, which have a readable difference, genetically speaking, from the native North American cougar. So Rusz and Swanson were able to rule out the Michigan cougar scats coming from escaped or released exotic pet pumas.

Ergo Rusz and Swanson's findings lend powerful credence to the theory of a naturally occurring and highly probable original, native population of cougars in Michigan rather than the animals being escaped or released ones from human captivity.

The doubters of the original/native population as source of the big cat might then ask: "If the Rusz and Swanson study shows a presence of cougars in Michigan, and they are not escaped or released pets, how'd they get here?" Are the cats wanderers from western states? After all, Michigan DNR officials sometimes cited this theory as possible along with the escaped/released pet explanation, claiming lonely males may have entered the state in search of a female partner.

Some years after Rusz's field work, verified by his and Swanson's DNA study showing conclusively the cougar to be in Michigan, much, much more indisputable evidence of the big cat's presence presented itself via numerous photos (mostly by trail cameras, as their usage increased) and track findings, subsequently authenticated by the Michigan DNR. Therefor the state agency has since largely dropped the escaped or released pet theory and substituted it with the wandering cat hypothesis.

However, the DNR of Michigan cannot be trusted (despite many of the agency's employees being honest and upright regarding *Felis concolor*). For years the organization denied the cougar's existence within the state, clinging firmly to the notion the big cat was eradicated in the early 1900s. As said, this was followed by statements that if there were a few around, they had to be escaped or released pets. Then the public and press were told, after the DNR was confronted with conclusive evidence via numerous pictures and other evidence showing the big cat to be present, that the animals must have migrated in from the west.

The DNR's explanation of and for the big cat's presence evolved over time as more and more proof came out. But we know for sure the agency has been deceptive, if not outright dishonest, over the years regarding the large feline. Consider the following:

An excellent photo of a cougar was taken in Alcona County in Michigan's Lower Peninsula in 1997. The mountain lion was witnessed on the property of then 83-year-old Larry Lippert. An employee of his, Jim Deutsch, snapped a picture of the cat relaxing in some ferns. The near-perfect image was shared with the Michigan DNR, who in short order concluded and stated the photo to be a hoax, as its agents claimed the cat was a dead specimen which had been stuffed by a taxidermist. Lippert was incensed at the accusation of trickery or outright fraud. However, the two men, Lippert and Deutsch, would soon enough be vindicated.

Department of Natural Resources officer Lawrence Robinson, in an email to colleagues dated July 15, 1998 (which was afterwards leaked and brought to public light), had this to say: "This is a note I absolutely dread writing. ... I had the terrible misfortune of seeing the Alcona Co. cougar. On July 6, I was picking up the bear baits on

This cougar photo was taken in the summer of 1997 by Jim Deutsch on the Alcona County, Michigan, property of his employer, Larry Lippert. *Photo courtesy of Dr. Patrick Rusz.*

routes in Alcona and Oscoda counties. It was pouring rain and I was soaked-ass wet and driving between bait sites. I was on a sandy, narrow USFS [United States Forest Service] road when I came over a rise and a cougar was in the road about 60 yards away. It immediately bolted into the brush. I stopped and looked at the fresh tracks. They were in soft sand and were very clear impressions showing the cat had been walking on the road toward me until I appeared. It angled across the trail taking a couple bounds before leaving the road.

"I did not have my camera in the truck to take pictures of the tracks. I drove to a gas station north of Comins and bought a little disposable Kodak camera. I returned to take pictures of the tracks and area … the pictures are good enough to show they are cat tracks. I used a folding knife and my boot track for a size reference in the photos.

"I told Glen [Matthews] about it and how reluctant I was to say

This cougar photo was taken on hunt club land in eastern Oscoda County, Michigan, in 1993. The location of the big cat was only four miles from the later 1997 Larry Lippert property picture. *Photo courtesy of Dr. Patrick Rusz.*

anything after dealing with Larry Lippert's picture last year. I still get letters and calls about the 'Alcona County Cougar.' Last year I was hounded by most of the news reporters in the state. … I have always been very skeptical about the cougar sightings we get from all over the state. So, you can understand why I wish this hadn't happened. … It was an adult animal and there were no other tracks around. I can't even give you a guess on weight, but the pictures show how deep the tracks were in comparison to my tracks.

"I figured I had to fess up eventually. What do I do to get the pictures and info to our division files without this getting out to the media? I really don't want this to turn into another media event like the picture last year did. Let me know your suggestions. By the way, the location is about 10 miles 'as the cougar flies' from the Lippert property where the picture was taken last summer."

A male motorist from Haslett, Michigan, photographed this cougar (at mailbox) through his windshield on the evening of June 21, 2017, while driving in Bath Township, Clinton County, in Michigan's Lower Peninsula. *Photo courtesy of Dr. Patrick Rusz.*

With an indisputable cover-up attempt by the state DNR having occurred, as evidenced by employee Robinson's email, a straightforward question may reasonably be asked: Why exactly has the DNR of Michigan engaged in so many past and ongoing attempts to minimize, or "pooh pooh," powerful evidence of the likelihood cougars never left the state—i.e., they were never completely wiped out? Your guess is as good as mine, but a particularly good theorization is that the agency does not want to have to spend a gigantic sum of money and mega resources setting up and running a cougar protection program due to the animal having been listed as endangered by the state. The truth will eventually come out.

In the meantime, Dr. Patrick Rusz and the Michigan Wildlife Conservancy remain convinced the modern cougars in Michigan to be from the continuous lineage of the state's original, native panther population (while allowing that some have indeed migrated in from western states).

This author too believes in both the "wandering in" and "original, native population" theories as explanations for the ongoing and current residing of *Felis concolor* within Michigan. Perhaps free-roaming cats from far western regions of the U.S. have always—from time to time—replenished or added to the state's long-surviving cougar stock. Why not?

Epilogue

Fake News and False Alarms

Within the prologue, mention was made of this epilogue. Why? Because any writer of nonfiction should do his or her due diligence to make sure the information presented is factual. I have tried to bring about the truth, but fully admit inaccuracies and mistakes may have been committed—but if so, honestly so. I would never conscientiously falsify or embellish material that I've put in print. To do so would be highly unethical, if not downright immoral.

Therefore, I bring you the following news stories as real-life historical examples of falsely reported, or incorrectly speculated, serious misdeeds committed against humans by the North American panther. This is done to prove that deliberate or honest misrepresentations exist and hopefully to thus exonerate myself if ever any of my book accounts prove false.

In early December 1900, numerous newspapers across Wisconsin and dozens more throughout the Midwestern United States printed a horrible and sickening story of an 8-year-old girl, a daughter of a man named C. F. Riley, being recently torn apart and consumed by a wild panther in the tiny western Wisconsin settlement of Mad Brook, not too far north of Eau Claire.

Being a wired article, every account of the reported tragedy was written almost verbatim from the original. All said the little girl was walking on a road near her family's farm when a panther leaped from the woods, seized the child in its "huge jaws" and carried the youngster into a swamp "where she met a most horrible death, being torn limb from limb. The few scattered remains were gathered up and buried."

The villagers quickly organized a panther hunt to exterminate all such brutes in the region. The avengers met with some success, as the story claimed a massive panther measuring 10 feet long from nose tip to tail tip was shot dead. Two other large (cats) were said to be seen by members of the hunt.

People near and far were jolted by the news of the girl's terrible fate. The initial shock soon gave way to both anger and sadness. It did not take very long, however, for many to learn the event never happened. The story turned out to be completely bogus.

Was the report fake due to an intentional, deliberate lie? Or was it accidentally false, due to some rumor that snowballed out of control? The answer to the question has not been determined, historically speaking. Some newspapers retracted the account upon learning it was indeed false, as they should have, because they were morally and ethically obligated to be truthful.

The *Vernon County Censor*, from the town of Viroqua, Wisconsin, published a retraction of the fake news story on the paper's front page, dated December 12, 1900. It was followed by a statement written from the pen of the false victim's father, dated December 9, 1900. They read:

"The CENSOR is gratified to learn that the report published in last week's issue, with reference to the killing of
C. F. Riley's little daughter by a panther, is unfounded. The
following letter from Mr. Riley will be read with rejoicing by
all of the friends of the family in this community:"

"Friend Munson:- We are very glad to tell you that the story
which has found its way into some of the papers about
our little daughter Blanchey being devoured by a panther,
is false. We desire to give our thanks for those well-meant
expressions of sympathy we have received by letter from
every source.

Very Respectfully,
C. F. Riley."

The *Cheboygan Democrat* of Cheboygan, Michigan, reported in its
April 30, 1898, edition that 52-year-old James McNeill, who lived
on and operated a little farm near Rogers City, Michigan, seemed
to have vanished from his home. The fellow was last seen nearly a
month earlier, on April 5, and was intoxicated. McNeill, a man physically disadvantaged, or "crippled," was suspected of having fallen
victim to a panther which was known to inhabit a thick swamp adjacent to his property.

After some investigation into the mystery of the farmer's whereabouts, on May 5, 1898, the *Presque Isle County Advance* of Rogers
City stated (with surname spelled slightly differently):

"Mr. James McNeil, of the Clay Banks, left home some months
or weeks ago without notifying his family as to where he was [going].
This caused reports to circulate [that] some disaster had befallen

[him]. When he did not turn up in a [week] or so, some one wrote a [ ] article to the Detroit Journal [and] Evening News stating that he thought that the panther, [which] for so many years frequented the large swamp back of his farm had devoured him …"

The article went on for some length, but concluded with: "It seems that Mr. McNeil has been all along working [at a] camp on the line of the D. M. road. He certainly left home [in an] eccentric manner; but Mrs. McNeil who knows his ways, has never offered the slightest alarm, knowing full well that he had gone to [pursue] work to support his family, and [not] to leave a home where no element of discord ever prevailed."

As mentioned, the latter example of a newspaper or two's false speculation or alarm that a panther had made prey of a human serves well to demonstrate how it is possible a researcher and an author (years later) could report a mistaken case as being real, if a correction statement was not found. That is, if one was ever even made in the first place.

On another note, it is interesting that both papers reported the inhabitance of a panther in the vicinity of the northern Lower Peninsula town of Rogers City, Michigan, as if it was common knowledge. The big cat's presence appears as nothing surprising or shocking to the communities of Cheboygan and Rogers City as late as 1898. The only excitement or curiosity seemed to be over whether or not the large, wild feline had killed and eaten the missing man.

To this day, credible sightings of panthers or cougars are reported from the wild terrain all around my hometown of Rogers City, Michigan, including near where the McNeil farm used to be—well over a hundred years later! Miles of dense swampland still abut that man's former property. I know this because it is part of the area I used to frequent while searching for massasauga rattlesnakes. The reptiles abound heavily in the region.

I have often wondered if maybe, just maybe, I'll one day bear witness to a massive-sized cat ambling through the same acreage—progeny of the McNeil farm panther of long, long ago.

Bibliography

Archival Material

Chase S. Osborn Papers, ca 1870–1949, Bentley Historical Library, University of Michigan, Boxes 15 & 104, Personal Letterbooks.
Pope, Vera, Transcriptionist, Berrien County Board [of] Supervisors Minutes, Williams & Hayden, January 24, 1939, page 4.

Books

Ballard, Ralph, *Tales of Early Niles*, R. Ballard, Niles, Michigan, 1948, page 96.
Baraga, Frederic, *A Dictionary of the Otchipwe Language* (reprinted in 1966), Ross & Haines, Inc., Minneapolis, Minnesota.

Burt, William H., *Mammals of the Great Lakes Region*, The University of Michigan Press, 1957, page 157.

Chapman, Chas. C. & Company, *History of Washtenaw County, Michigan: and Biographies of Representative Citizens*, C. C. Chapman and Company, 1881.

Ellis, Franklin, *History of Berrien & Van Buren Counties, Michigan*, Philadelphia: D.W. Ensign & Co., 1880, page 502.

Ellis, Franklin, *History of Genesee County, Michigan*, Philadelphia: Everts & Abbott, 1879, pages 197, 198.

Fields, Armond, *Katharine Dexter McCormick: Pioneer for Women's Rights*, Greenwood Publishing Group, 2003, pages 5, 276.

Johnson, Crisfield, *History of Branch County, Michigan*, Philadelphia: Everts & Abbott, 1879, page 225.

Mathews, Alfred, *History of Cass County, Michigan*, Chicago: Waterman, Watkins & Co., 1882, page 303.

Portrait and Biographical Record of Genesee, Lapeer and Tuscola Counties, Michigan, Chicago: Chapman Brothers, 1892, pages 837, 838.

Stannard, Mrs. Julia Dexter, "Address Before the Washtenaw County Pioneer Society, June 12, 1895," *Michigan Pioneer and Historical Collections*, Vol. 28, 1897 & 1898, pages 565, 566.

Magazine Articles

LaPointe, Dave, "The Cat That Isn't," *Michigan Natural Resources Magazine*, January–February 1978, pages 28–30.

Maki, Don, "Cougars: U.P. Big Cat Sightings Include Reports of Cubs," *U.P. Outdoors*, Saturday, September 25, 1993.

Newspaper Articles

"A Camp Scourge," *Presque Isle County Advance* (Rogers City, Michigan), January 4, 1883, page 1.

"A Child Rescued From a Panther," *Fort Wayne Weekly Sentinel* (Fort Wayne, Indiana), September 29, 1875, page 3.

"A Horrible Fate," *Stevens Point Journal* (Stevens Point, Wisconsin), December 4, 1900, page 2.

"A Little Child Killed By A Wildbeast In Illinois," *New Albany Daily Ledger* (New Albany, Indiana), August 1, 1863, page 1.

"A Panther Eats Up A Little Boy," *Macon Georgia Weekly Telegraph And Georgia Journal And Messenger*, July 5, 1870, page 2.

"An Osceola Wild Cat," *Isabella County Enterprise* (Mt. Pleasant, Michigan), January 5, 1900, page 5.

"Baby Killed By A Panther," *Logansport Pharos Tribune* (Logansport, Indiana), June 27, 1892, page 1.

"Carried Off By A Panther," *Macon Weekly Telegraph* (Macon, Georgia), July 20, 1892, page 4.

Charlevoix County Herald (East Jordan, Michigan), November 17, 1916, page 5.

Cheboygan Democrat (Cheboygan, Michigan), April 30, 1898, page 4.

"Child Killed By A Panther," *Logansport Journal* (Logansport, Indiana), August 26, 1854, page 1.

"Claims Panther Attacks Cattle And Kills Sheep," *Belding Banner* (Belding, Michigan), September 21, 1921, page 1.

"Could It Be Gogomain Ghost?" *The Evening News* (Sault Ste. Marie, Michigan), Monday, November 27, 1972, page 4.

Crawford Avalanche (Grayling, Michigan), August 16, 1894, page 4.

Crawford Avalanche (Grayling, Michigan), September 8, 1892, page 3.

"Depict County's Lore in Parade," *Courier-Northerner* (Paw Paw, Michigan), October 4 [or October 11], 1929.

"Fight With a Panther in Florida," *Madison Wisconsin State Journal*, December 3, 1869, page 2.

"Gigantic Panther Slain," *The Daily News* (Marshall, Michigan), November 28, 1899, page 4.

Indianapolis Evening Journal (Indianapolis, Indiana), March 23, 1872.

Isabella County Enterprise (Mt. Pleasant, Michigan), August 14, 1878.

Isabella County Enterprise (Mt. Pleasant, Michigan), January 7, 1880, page 5.

Isabella County Enterprise (Mt. Pleasant, Michigan), December 24, 1886, pages 6 & 8.

Ivins, Delbert S., "It Was No Ghost: Thrilling Adventure in a Michigan Forest," *Gladwin County Record* (Cedar, Michigan), November 7, 1890, page 7.

"Killed Big Catamount," *Sault Ste. Marie News* (Sault Ste. Marie, Michigan), January 3, 1907.

"Killed By A Panther," *Democratic Expounder and Calhoun County Patriot* (Marshall, Michigan), March 19, 1874.

"Killed by a Panther," *Rochester Daily Republican* (Rochester, Indiana), November 26, 1892, Page 1.

Lohrer, Lydia, "Outdoors: Reports of Cougars in Lower Peninsula Are Nothing New," *Detroit Free Press*, July 9, 2017.

New Albany Democrat (New Albany, Indiana), September 16, 1847, page 2.

Oosting, Jonathon, "Cougar Verified for first time in Lower Peninsula," *The Detroit News*, June 29, 2017.

"Panther Fight," *Jacksonville Republican* (Jacksonville, Alabama), June 1, 1837, page 4.

"Panther Kills Two Children," *Marshall County Independent* (Plymouth, Indiana), November 30, 1900, page 2.

"Panther Overleaped His Prey: An Ugly Scar That Testifies to a Hunter's Narrow Escape," *Savannah Morning News* (Savannah, Georgia), October 25, 1896, page 26.

"Peninsular State News," *Newberry News* (Newberry, Michigan), November 1, 1895, page 6.

Pontiac Gazette (Pontiac, Michigan), December 24, 1886, page 6.

Presque Isle County Advance (Rogers City, Michigan), February 16, 1882, page 2.

Presque Isle County Advance (Rogers City, Michigan), May 5, 1898, page 1.

Rintamaki, George, "Outdoor Observations: 'Mystery Cat,'" *Upper Peninsula Sunday Times*, October 22, 1978, C-3.

South Haven Sentinel (South Haven, Michigan), August 22, 1896, page 1.

South Haven Sentinel (South Haven, Michigan), January 28, 1882, page 1.

St. Joseph Herald (St. Joseph, Michigan), January 23, 1875.

Stoll, Albert, Jr., "A Panther in Michigan," *Ironwood Daily Globe* (Ironwood, Michigan), November 20, 1933, page 4.

The Alma Record (Alma, Michigan), February 12, 1897, page 3.

"The Report Was Untrue," *Vernon County Censor* (Viroqua, Wisconsin), December 12, 1900, page 1.

Thorntown Argus (Thorntown, Indiana), December 1, 1894, page 6.

"Trappers See Huge Animal," *The Holland Evening Sentinel* (Holland, Michigan), April 10, 1958, page 7.

True Northerner (Paw Paw, Michigan), January 31, 1913, page 1.

"Under the Courthouse Steeple," *The Ironwood Times* (Ironwood, Michigan), April 16, 1941.

Yoder, Nelson, "50 years of buck tails recalled by veteran deer-hunter, Tony Schild of Kneeland," *Oscoda County News* (Mio, Michigan), November 26, 1981, page 5.

Yoder, Nelson, "Additional big cat sightings by long-time residents indicate cats may have always been here," *Oscoda County News* (Mio, Michigan), November 18, 1982, page 3.

Yoder, Nelson, "Big cat tales commonplace among long time residents of Oscoda County," *Oscoda County News* (Mio, Michigan), December 24, 1981, page 5.

Yoder, Nelson, "Observers of the 'Big Cat' agree—seeing and hearing makes you a believer," *Oscoda County News* (Mio, Michigan), November 11, 1982, page 3.

Online

"Dexter, Judge Samuel W., House," Michigan State Housing Development Authority: Historic Sites Online. Archived from the original on April 21, 2013.

Historic District Study Committee (September 10, 2001), *Gordon Hall*, (PDF), Washtenaw County.

Hopkins Burns Design Studio (August 2011), *Gordon Hall Rehabilitation Master Plan*, (PDF), Washtenaw County.

John C. Rinehart and Parthena (Lawson) Rinehart, www. findagrave. com, retrieved on August 18, 2022.

Michigan Department of Natural Resources, Wildlife Division, Internal Memo (email), Robinson, Lawrence, July 15, 1998.

Yancy, F. Orla (June 30, 1937), "Judge Samuel W. Dexter House," (PDF) *Historic American Buildings Survey*, Washington, D.C.: Library of Congress. Archived from the original (PDF) on October 29, 2013.

Professional Papers

Foster, Donald W., and Donald R. Hagge, M.D., "A Unique Secondary Burial of Four Children Found in Taymouth

Township, Saginaw County, Michigan," *Michigan Archaeologist*, Vol. 21, No. 2, 1975, pages 63–70.

Manville, Richard H., "The Vertebrate Fauna of the Huron Mountains, Michigan," *The American Midland Naturalist*, Vol. 39, No. 3, 1948, pages 615 & 634.

Rusz, Patrick J., Ph.D., and Bradley J. Swanson, "Detection and Classification of Cougars in Michigan Using Low Copy DNA Sources," *The American Midland Naturalist*, Vol. 155, No. 2, 2006, pages 363–372.

Rusz, Patrick J., Ph.D., "The Cougar In Michigan: Sightings And Related Information," (A Technical Publication of the Bengel Wildlife Center), 2001, page 29.

Wood, N. A., and L. R. Dice, "Records of the Distribution of Michigan Mammals," *Michigan Academy of Science, Arts and Letters*, Papers, 1924, 3:425–469.

About the Author

Aaron Veselenak was born and raised in Rogers City, Michigan, but now hails from nearby Ocqueoc Township, Presque Isle County, Michigan. As a lover of nature and history, Veselenak has often combined both subjects in his writings. Mr. Veselenak is a K–12 substitute teacher and has been a house painter for more than three decades.

In addition, after obtaining a master's degree in political science (with minors in history and economics), he taught American government and history as an adjunct instructor at Alpena Community College, Alpena, Michigan, for 25 years. Over time the author has written several historical articles which have been published in various periodicals. His only other book is *Swamp Rattler: Facts, History and Status of Michigan's Sole Venomous Serpent.*

About the Artist

Luann Kuznicki was born in Rogers City, Michigan, but now resides near Midland, Michigan. Her love of nature, gardening, and art started at an early age. Luann's parents encouraged their daughter to continue with her passion for art by enrolling the young woman into college-level courses via mail at the Minnesota Art Institute while she was a teen. She took art classes in high school and college, though ended up choosing science as an official career path and became a high school teacher. However, the artist within Luann was creatively utilized within her chemistry, biology, and anatomy and physiology instruction.

Ms. Kuznicki retired in 2020 after 30 years of teaching and was therefore able to pursue her artsy side to an even greater extent. She enjoys many different mediums and uses her own dried flowers and other plants in some of her resin creations. Oil paints, acrylics, and the simple but mighty pencil are all put to use. Luann owns her own online business named "Lulu's Innovative Art."

www.ingramcontent.com/pod-product-compliance
Lightning Source LLC
Chambersburg PA
CBHW070115030426
42335CB00016B/2159